Paris

Jarrold Publishing

CONTENTS

Introducing Paris	3
Essential details in brief	7
Cityscapes	8
Phases of history	10
What Paris has to offer	12–42
Everyday life in Paris – Some distinctive features – Palaces and parks – Architecture – Museums and exhibitions – Food and drink – The vocabulary of eating and drinking – Historic places – Opera, theatre and the concert hall – Paris by night – Haute couture and fashion – Shopping	
Suggested tours of the city	
Around the Place de l'Opéra	43
The Marais	46
The Triumphal Way: Louvre – Tuileries – Concorde – Champs-Elysées – Place de l'Etoile (Charles-de-Gaulle)	48
The Louvre (palace, museum and pyramid)	51
The islands in the Seine	53
The Latin Quarter and St-Germain-des-Prés	57
Paris – a classified directory	59–82
Beyond the city: selected excursions	82–88
Versailles, Malmaison, St-Germain-en-Laye, Fontainebleau	84–88
Other châteaux	88
Cathedrals	88
Useful things to know	89
Maps	
Paris – cityscapes	8/9
The environs of Paris	82/83
Paris – principal sights	back cover
Index	95–96

Title page: Notre-Dame

Palais de Chaillot from the Eiffel Tower

Introducing Paris

On your first visit to Paris, you would naturally like an answer to the question: what is Paris like? If you have been there before, the question would be: how has Paris changed? What does this city, which is developing rapidly to meet the challenges of the next millennium, look like at the moment?

A brief look through the first chapter of this guide will tell you a great deal. At least you will know where you are. Before doing anything else, go into the nearest café or bistro. Find yourself a seat from which you can see all there is to be seen, carefully choose your drink – a cup of coffee, an aperitif, a glass of wine or whatever else takes your fancy – and relax. You will soon feel yourself starting to unwind; you will begin to realise that no problem is insoluble...

Understanding Paris can be a life's work: as a historical entity that has grown up over thousands of years, as the centre of political power in a proud nation, as a cultural centre of the Old World, as a city of art, as a symbol of the art of living. And yet Paris is a city which is incomparably easy to live in, a city on a human scale which is closed to nobody, not even the casual visitor. It is true that it takes months and even years really to get to know Paris. Yet you can fall in love with the place in an hour. Paris is undoubtedly one of the best-loved cities in the world. Other great cities, such as New York, Tokyo, Moscow and London, have their devotees, but for many of their inhabitants as well as their visitors they do have their nightmare elements. So why is it that Paris has hardly any enemies in the world? Perhaps you will find the answer in the following pages.

The price of progress

After Baron Haussmann had driven his boulevards through the city, the magnificent buildings of the *Belle Epoque* had been built and the Métro first began to rattle in all directions under the city's streets, Paris changed very little for many decades. For a long time, modernity was banished to the outer districts of the city and the *banlieue*, or suburbs. Nine-tenths of the outer regions of the conurbation, which have a population of ten million, have nothing to offer but the ugly anonymity of ghost towns, residential wastelands, brutalist architecture, consumer bunkers and nightmarish traffic systems.

In the meantime, even in the historic city centre, the wounds have become more painful. For example, les Halles, the markets that were the legendary 'belly of Paris', have been transferred to the suburb of Rungis; motorways have been driven through the city and several architectural gems have been torn down, to be replaced by skyscrapers which, with an embarrassing lack of success, try to compete with the Eiffel Tower. Sensitive Parisians can only stand by as their city, the capital of *haute cuisine*, is remorselessly taken over by fast-food restaurant chains. The need for the new projects remains a controversial issue, as witness the case of *La Grande Arche* (The Great Arch) at La Défense, which completes the city's grandiose east–west axis. On the other hand, these massive building projects are evidence of the astonishing vitality of a city which is now 2,000 years old. The once shocking Pompidou Centre, and the Musée d'Orsay, installed in the old Gare d'Orsay, have long since been accepted, and the same is to be expected of the pyramid in the Louvre and the new Bastille opera house.

A metropolis with charm

While many cities have lost their character in the recent past, Paris has without doubt remained the city so dearly loved throughout the world. It is still possible to buy a joint of meat here on a Sunday morning, to browse in second-hand bookshops until midnight, and dine in a restaurant at one o'clock in the morning. At whatever time you might want a nightcap, a bar in the neighbourhood is certain to be open. More than 100,000 people – cooks, waiters, barkeepers, waitresses, cabaret dancers and others – are in the business of providing their fellow citizens with their comforts at any time of the day or night. Of course this gives rise to certain very real economic and social problems. Nevertheless, it is possible to live more freely in Paris than in many other, more highly regulated cities.

Naturally, the famous sights of Paris are among its greatest attractions to visitors. And yet Paris is not merely a collection of monuments and museums, but essentially a city that can satisfy all the senses. Even if you are here for the first time and can stay only two or three days, do not allow yourself to be tyrannised by a sightseeing programme. Go for a short walk through one of the old quarters of the city, along the Seine, or on the Île St-Louis. Sit on a bench in the Luxembourg Gardens or the Tuileries. Experience the atmosphere of the Latin Quarter and the Place de la Bastille. Have a drink in the bar on the nearest street corner or in the Café de la Paix. Spend some time choosing a good restaurant for dinner. Go window-shopping, whether in the elegant or the popular shopping streets, and go for a ride on the Métro, even if you can afford to take a taxi.

The Great Arch at La Défense

Art Nouveau entrance to the Palais Royal Métro station

Café de la Paix

Paris – 'city of love'

Parisian reserve – and Parisian passion

Most visitors to the city will feel little more than lookers-on. The Parisians are city-dwellers *par excellence*: tolerant to the point of indifference, they are not interested in other people, however important they may be in their own country. This indifference is typical of inveterate city-dwellers the world over; in this respect, Parisians are no different from Londoners or New Yorkers. Only those who are sociable and conversant with the French language can count on being allowed to join in a little.

One stereotype seems to be ineradicable: Paris – the greatest hotbed of vice in the world! There are undoubtedly many cities in which sin flourishes more abundantly than in Paris. However, the misconception has historical roots. It is true that the upper classes in France, from the kings of the Renaissance period to the bons viveurs of the *Belle Epoque*, were often excessively depraved. But to be able to act in that way it was necessary to be powerful or very rich. In the relatively prudish French Republic, all that has remained is a sort of mass-produced commodity, such as the striptease shows (not only in Montmartre), which differ from similar shows in Hamburg and London only in extravagance and quantity. Parisians generally go to them only when they feel obliged to take visitors from the provinces. By and large they are tourist traps, offering inferior champagne at inflated prices to audiences that watch politely as the spectacle on stage presents the opportunity, twice in an evening, to experience vicariously the 'hotbed of vice'. In this respect it is enlightening, and sobering, to remember that twice as many cookery books are sold each year in France as are books on the art of love.

Paris is the city of love rather than of vice, when all is said and done. At this point, it is impossible to avoid mentioning the Parisian couples whose love for each other is more openly and passionately expressed than anywhere else in the world: in the parks, on the streets and even on the escalators in department stores. And it is not only the young ones who act like that. An aura of tenderness lies over the whole city, encompassing all generations.

So if it is at all possible, do not come to Paris alone! Come with someone you love or whose company you enjoy. For that is the other side to this passionate, convivial city: on your own, you can feel very lonely.

Essential details in brief

Importance: Even in the Middle Ages, regarded as the centre of France. Position reinforced under the Bourbons.

Population: City: approximately 2.2 million in 105 sq km. Paris region (28 municipalities): 10 million in about 12,000 sq km. Annual growth rate: over 125,000. Almost 19% of the total population of France live in this 2.2% of its surface area. Population density in the suburbs: 820 inhabitants per sq km; in the city: almost 22,000 per sq km – it is one of the most densely populated regions in the world. Large number of foreigners: 20% of the population in the Paris region born abroad, principally Algerians, Tunisians, Moroccans, Portuguese and Italians.

Administration: Paris region: 7 *départements*. The City of Paris is the Département Ville de Paris (with a mayor), divided into 20 *arrondissements*, or districts, each with 4 quarters. Their numeration follows a spiral, working out clockwise from the centre (Louvre).

Institutions: Seat of the president of the Republic and of the government (the National Assembly and the Senate), and of international organisations (UNESCO, OECD); diplomatic missions of sovereign states; seat of the Catholic archbishop and of the head of the Russian Orthodox Church in Europe.

Industry: In the Paris region, 23% of industrial production, 28% of all industrial employment in France. Main industries: optical industries, automobile and aircraft manufacture and electrical industry; 'Articles de Paris' (about 60,000 workers): haute couture, perfumery, jewellery, etc.

Traffic: End point of 3 motorways, 23 trunk roads and all long-distance railway routes. Airports: Orly and Roissy-Charles-de-Gaulle.

Inland shipping: Third largest port, after Marseilles and Le Havre: 60 km of quays, spread over the waterways network of the Seine, Marne, Oise and several canals in the Paris region.

Cityscapes

The cityscape of Paris, like that of so many cities, is determined by a river: the Seine flows in a broad arc from east to west through the city. The Île de la Cité which lies in the river was the heart of the historic settlement, which spread first to the left (south) bank and then to the right (north) bank of the Seine.

Right Bank: The right bank of the Seine is today by far the larger and more important. Here are most of the historic monuments, the prestige buildings and the shopping centres, and the major residential and industrial districts. One particular feature that makes Paris a world-class metropolis is the traffic axis which runs from east to west through the whole city, from the Place de la Bastille via the Rue de Rivoli, Place de la Concorde, Champs-Elysées and Place de l'Etoile to the satellite city of La Défense, and includes the Louvre and the Tuileries.

Left Bank: The left bank of the Seine cannot offer anything comparable. With the Latin Quarter and the Sorbonne, St-Germain-des-Prés and Montparnasse, it has traditionally been considered an area of students and intellectuals, artists and bohemians, but is inhabited predominantly by ordinary mortals.

To the north the Butte Montmartre, crowned by the Basilica of Sacré-Coeur, rises 100 m above Paris.

To the south are the lower hills of Ste-Geneviève and Montparnasse, which play virtually no role in the cityscape.

The overall impression of Paris is of a gigantic, stone-grey sea of buildings which, at the city boundary, merges almost imperceptibly with the countless suburbs surrounding the city.

Bois de Vincennes and Bois de Boulogne: These two parks (to the east and west respectively) have survived as large green areas, with lakes.

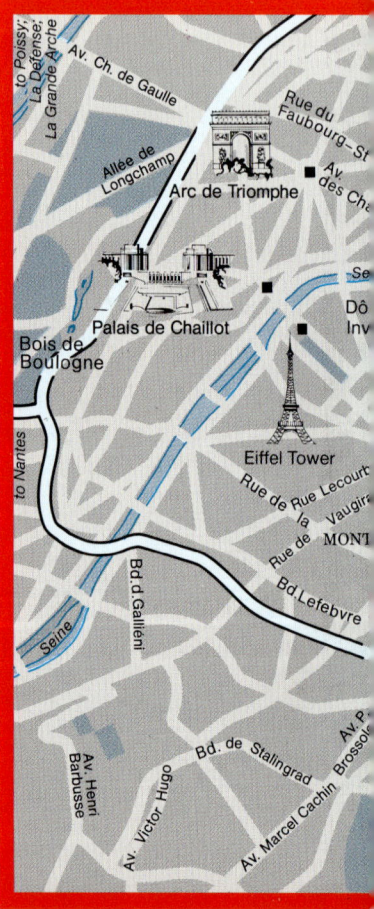

Cityscapes 9

Phases of history

Gauls, Romans and Gallo-Romans

The island in the Seine known today as the Île de la Cité was inhabited in prehistoric times. The Parisii, a Celtic tribe, are thought to have founded a trading centre there, which they called *Lutuhezi*, as early as the 3rd c. BC. During the Roman conquest of Gaul Lutuhezi was partly destroyed; later, however, under its Roman name of *Lutetia Parisiorum*, it again became an important trading centre and began to expand on to the left bank of the Seine. Around AD 280, it was destroyed by Germanic tribes.

Dionysius and Geneviève

According to legend, the first bishop of Lutetia was a man called Dionysius (Denis), who was martyred around AD 250 (on Montmartre – *Mons Martyrum*, or Martyrs' Hill). In AD 360 Lutetia became known as Paris. In AD 451 Attila the Hun, on his campaign of conquest through Europe, invaded Gaul and threatened Paris. Legend has it that a nun called Geneviève averted disaster through the power of prayer. Astonishingly, Attila's hordes suddenly changed direction and headed south; in 452 they were crushed by the Romans and Visigoths at the Catalaunian Fields. Geneviève subsequently became the patron saint of Paris.

Merovingians and Carolingians

In 486 the king of the Franks, Clovis I, the grandson of Merovius, conquered Paris and shortly afterwards made it his capital. He built his residence on the Île de la Cité. Paris became the most important city north of the Alps. In the 8th c. Charlemagne, the king of the Franks, transferred his seat of government from Paris to Aix-la-Chapelle. Paris lost its central position, and during the course of the 9th c. was devastated several times by Scandinavian or Norse pirates, who in their Viking ships pushed deep into France along the Seine. In 888 the Franks elected Odo, Count of Paris, to be king of France after his successful defence of Paris against the fifth attack by marauding Norsemen.

987

A key date: Hugues Capet became king of France. Under his rule and that of his successors, Paris became the undisputed capital of France, and its rulers accumulated more and more power for themselves. Paris was now expanding on to the right bank of the Seine. At the beginning of the 12th c., work began on the construction of the great abbey church of St-Denis, and in 1163 the cathedral of Notre-Dame was started. Philippe II (Philippe Auguste, 1180–1223) had the city enclosed by a wall, the fortress of the Louvre built and the wooden bridges over the Seine replaced by stone ones. During his reign, the population of Paris grew to 100,000 and the city was said to be the largest and most beautiful in Europe. Under his successor, Louis IX (St Louis), several theological colleges were founded on the left bank of the Seine, the most famous of which was the Sorbonne, founded in 1253 on the Mont Ste-Geneviève.

The House of Valois

In the late Middle Ages, the increasingly powerful and self-confident citizens of Paris were causing major difficulties for the kings of France. The Hundred Years War between England and France weakened the country. Despite the extension of its fortifications in 1370, Paris fell to the English in 1420 and was not freed until 1437, by Charles VII, after an

Palais de Justice

assault led by Joan of Arc had been repelled. After the reunification of France, Paris expanded further, but the French kings preferred to stay away from the permanently turbulent capital. They resided in their châteaux on the Loire or at nearby Fontainebleau. After the Massacre of St Bartholomew in 1572, when about 3,000 Protestant Huguenots were killed, peace was not restored to the city for a long time.

The House of Bourbon

Henri IV, the first king of the House of Bourbon, made his peace with Paris after his conversion to Catholicism, having abjured his faith, so it is said, with the cynical remark that 'Paris is worth a mass'. In 1594 the gates of the city were opened to him. Under the Bourbon kings the city continued to grow. Around the middle of the 17th c. the city had about 500,000 inhabitants. Louis XIV, the 'Sun King', transferred his court to Versailles, from where the strings of European politics were pulled; nevertheless, during his reign, the still essentially medieval fortified city was transformed into an open one, criss-crossed by new roads.

The Napoleonic period

The French Revolution, which began in 1789 with the storming of the Bastille, took place for the most part in Paris, which was also the centre of Napoleon's increasing power during his numerous wars. This period came to an end after the occupation of Paris by the victorious Russians, Prussians and Austrians.

Between 1815 and 1914

In spite of all the power struggles and revolutions, Paris continued to grow into a magnificent city. Most of the credit for its development should go to Napoleon III (1852–70) and his prefect Baron Haussmann. The Franco-Prussian War (1870–71), during which Paris was occupied by German troops, only briefly interrupted the irresistible rise of the city, which reached its peak around the turn of the century in the cultivated decadence of the *Belle Epoque*.

From 1914 to the present

With the outbreak of the First World War 'the lights went out in Europe'. Although Paris suffered little physical damage during the two great wars of the 20th c., other world cities – London, New York and from time to time Berlin – challenged its leading position. Between 1940 and 1944 Paris was occupied by German troops. The city experienced its last two crises after the military coup in Algeria in 1958, which brought General de Gaulle to power, and with the 'May Revolution' of 1968, triggered by unrest among students.

What Paris has to offer

The following pages put Paris 'on display'. You should make first acquaintance here and briefly review the possibilities so that you may make plans according to your inclination. You will find in the following sections, 'Suggested tours of the city' and 'Paris – a classified directory', the necessary practical help.

Market stalls in the Latin Quarter

Everyday life in Paris

Left Bank: On the left bank of the Seine, opposite the *Île de la Cité* and the *Île St-Louis*, is 'the other Paris', as it says in the picture books: couples who seem even more closely entwined with each other than in other parts of the city; anglers who, undaunted, still cast their lines into the polluted waters of the Seine, despite the obvious lack of fish in the area; *bouquinistes* in front of their bookstands along the embankments of the Seine, who obviously do not care whether any of the people browsing among their wares actually want to buy anything. And under the bridges over the Seine, there are certainly still a few *clochards*, tramps who carry all their worldly possessions around with them. After a long period of little change, their numbers are beginning to increase considerably; this is a social phenomenon, no longer restricted to Paris, which on closer acquaintance soon loses its romantic aspects. The fact remains that the Parisian tramps have the advantage over their colleagues in other countries in originality, and sometimes also in philosophical depth.

The Latin Quarter: Something is always happening in the traditional student quarter. Much of the activity has been concentrated of late in the narrow streets around the church of *St-Séverin*, which are closed to traffic in the evenings. In the hours leading up to midnight, these streets resound to the noise of buskers, playing as well, and as loud, as individual talents permit. If you are lucky, a fiery steel band will play something for you. But you may also come across a solo clarinettist giving his best rendition of a Schubert piece – at least that's the name on the sheet music; the delicate sound of the instrument is lost in the general clamour. A restless, seething throng of people moves through the streets, and fire-eaters draw large crowds. As do political speakers . . . in 1968, not far from here, students and police engaged in bloody battles. Paris is a city with two faces.

Barrel organ at the Pompidou Centre

St-Germain-des-Prés

You will not find the main square of this district on the map, because it has no name. Here, five streets meet – Rue Dauphine, Rue Mazarine, Rue de Buci, Rue St-André-des-Arts and Rue de l'Ancienne Comédie – and several cars collide every day. The street cafés afford wonderful views of the populous scene – a particular mixture of Parisian intellectuals and bohemians, interspersed with middle-class residents of the neighbourhood.

Rue Mouffetard

In contrast, the scene here is lower-middle-class and picturesque. This is one of the most distinctive streets in Paris and has survived astonishingly well. As you push past the brightly coloured, aromatic displays, you will certainly regret your inability to shop as selectively and bargain as hard as the determined local housewives. Incidentally, the *Rue de Buci*, mentioned above, is a similarly appetising and lively street for food shopping, with the slightly intellectual atmosphere of the St-Germain district. But if you are looking for something more ordinary and less refined, try the *Rue Lepic* in Montmartre.

Shopping in the Rue Mouffetard

Some distinctive features

For addresses see pages 59–61

Eiffel Tower and Trocadéro fountains

The Eiffel Tower is the trademark of Paris. Contemporaries of its designer, Gustave Eiffel, were much exercised by the question of whether it was beautiful or ugly, useful or redundant. Today, the whole world has grown accustomed to the 'highest curiosity in the world'. A lift will take you to the first platform (57 m, restaurant), the second platform (115 m, restaurant) and the third platform (300 m, panoramic view). On foot, you will have to climb up 1,652 steps! Standing centrally under the tower will give you a marvellous impression of the elegance of the structure, which weighs 7,000 tonnes. The tower celebrated its 100th birthday in 1989 (see page 66).

Père Lachaise Cemetery is not only the largest in Paris, but also a fantastic labyrinth of monumental sepulchral architecture. The array of temples and chapels, towers and minarets, columns and statuettes, angels, apostles and gods of antiquity commissioned by mourning friends and relatives in the 19th c. constitutes a veritable museum of grotesque lapses of taste. Those buried here include the famous lovers Abelard and Héloïse, Chopin, Oscar Wilde, Marcel Proust, Modigliani and Edith Piaf. In May 1871, the last pocket of Communard resistance held out in the cemetery. The 147 survivors of the carnage among the graves were shot against the cemetery wall.

Montmartre Cemetery is smaller and more intimate. Among those buried here are Zola, Berlioz, Degas and Offenbach.

The Canal St-Martin links the Canal de l'Ourcq with the Seine; it is used by about 4,000 barges each year. In the lower stretches, where it flows in part above street level, it is controlled by locks, crossed by high footbridges and shaded by old trees. It is a charming area, 'a corner of Holland under the Parisian sky'.

Montmartre, the 'Martyrs' Hill' (see page 10), is indeed a hill, rising 100 metres above the Seine and offering a splendid view over the city, particularly at night. On top of the hill stands the *Basilica of Sacré-Coeur*, whose kitschy, wedding-cake style of architecture has been so often derided that one could almost feel sorry for it. On the slopes facing the city, a few secluded corners and squares (*Place Emile Goudeau*) and romantic flights of steps have survived, and on the other side of the hill there is even a real vineyard.

Montmartre today lives principally on memories of its great bohemian period between 1871 and 1900, when artists

Artist in Montmartre

and writers such as Renoir, Toulouse-Lautrec, Picasso, Braque, Juan Gris, Utrillo, Apollinaire and Max Jacob, to name only the most famous, lived or worked there. Of the places they frequented then, the *Moulin Rouge*, Toulouse-Lautrec's favourite haunt, and the *Lapin Agile*, a meeting place for Picasso, Utrillo and their friends, survive to this day.

Café life, Montmartre

Paris from the slopes below the Sacré-Coeur

The countless daubers in the *Place du Tertre*, seeking fortune rather than fame with their mass-produced work, are but a pale, commercialised echo of that great bohemian period. In the morning, before the activity starts, the square is tolerably picturesque. The same is true of the narrow streets through which the boulevards at the foot of the hill can be reached; it is here, between *Place Pigalle* and *Place Clichy*, that 'the sinful life' is acted out every night for the benefit of tourists (see pages 35–37 and 76–77).

Montparnasse, virtually unrecognisable now as a hill, is today one of the great nightclub districts of Paris, with rather more of an intellectual element than Montmartre – it is, after all, on the Left Bank. Its great period began when the bohemians moved there from Montmartre around the turn of the century. It ended with the Second World War. The painters Modigliani, Chagall and Léger, the sculptors Zadkine and Archipenko, the composers Stravinsky, Honegger and Milhaud, the writers Breton, Cocteau, Apollinaire and Hemingway, and even Lenin and Trotsky are the district's spiritual heroes. Today, people are less demanding. The bright life is concentrated in the short section of the *Boulevard Montparnasse* between the *Rue de Rennes* and the *Boulevard Raspail*, where such celebrated cafés-restaurants as *La Coupole*, *Le Dôme* and *La Rotonde* are located. Slightly further west, near the *Gare Maine-Montparnasse*, a modern commercial and residential district has emerged, symbolised by the *Tour Maine-Montparnasse*, which dominates the entire district and is, at 210 m, the highest skyscraper in Europe (by night it is a blaze of lights).

Palaces and parks

For addresses see pages 62–64

Palais Royal: Outside, the roar of the traffic in the Avenue de l'Opéra and the Rue de Rivoli. Inside, the peace and tranquillity of a monastery cloister somewhere in the provinces. One has to become aware of the contrast in order to enjoy it. The old palace was built in 1632 as an elegant residence for Cardinal Richelieu; after his death it was occupied by Philippe d'Orléans, the brother of Louis XIV. It was here that Philippe held the infamous orgies about which his wife, Henriette d'Angleterre, complained so bitterly in her letters. After 1780, under Philippe-Egalité, the garden was surrounded on the three remaining sides by arcades and residential buildings, which became the favourite meeting places of both aristocratic and revolutionary circles. It has sustained serious damage on several occasions, but has now been restored. Today, the palace is the seat of the French Council of State, and the arcade shops are now occupied by dealers in stamps, medals and curios; their idyllic, slightly sleepy surroundings match the atmosphere of the garden itself. One is also aware of the relaxing effect engendered by the almost musical harmony of the structure.

The Palais Royal

Jardin du Luxembourg

Palais and Jardin du Luxembourg: The palace was built in 1615 for Maria de' Medici, the widow of Henri IV, in the Tuscan style of her native country, combined with the traditional forms of the French Renaissance. The palace, which today is the seat of the French Senate, provides the imposing backdrop for the enchanting Luxembourg Gardens, a playground for the children of the Latin Quarter, who can sail their boats on the lake or watch the puppet theatre. It is also a favourite haunt of students, who flirt here or simply sit down to read a book in peace. Finally, it is an oasis for elderly people, who sit on the park chairs, blinking in the sun, reading a newspaper, playing chess, knitting or simply contemplating the world. You should not fail to imbibe the very Parisian atmosphere of these gardens, so often described and praised.

Bois de Boulogne: The park, spread over an area of 900 ha in the west of the city, is a stroke of luck for Parisians, since Paris has few large green areas. It has not been a real wood for a long time; rather it is a recreation area, with many paths for riding and walking, all too many roads (unfortunately), sports facilities, the two racecourses of Auteuil and Longchamp, restaurants and pavilions. If you do not wish simply to wander through the Bois, you can take a walk of about one hour round the idyllic artificial lake (*Lac Inférieur*), where you can also hire rowing boats. If you have more time, go to the *Parc du Pré Catelan* with its huge copper beech and the adjoining open-air theatre. You can eat very well in the *Pavillon Royal* on the Lac Inférieur or in the Pré Catelan. Or it may be more fun to picnic in the sweet-smelling meadows.

Parc Bagatelle: a sort of appendix to the Bois, with elegant grounds and enchanting displays of flowers — narcissi, tulips and roses.

Architecture

For addresses see pages 65–70

Apart from *Notre-Dame* and the *Sainte-Chapelle*, which will be considered more closely on one of the tours, Paris can be enjoyed without any further church visits. But those who are interested in medieval church architecture should see the former abbey church and royal mausoleum of St-Denis, St-Eustache and also St-Germain-l'Auxerrois.

St-Denis: When St Denis was beheaded on Montmartre at the end of the 3rd c., the martyr is said to have picked up his head and walked to the place where he wished to be buried. He was buried at the spot where he collapsed. As a result of the pilgrimage to his grave, a church and later a massive Benedictine abbey were built on the site. The church that stands here today was begun by Abbot Suger in 1137, and was consecrated in 1281. It was at St-Denis that elements of the Gothic style (on the façade, in the porch and in the choir) first appeared. In simple terms, the French Gothic style spread from here throughout the Île de France and later throughout the whole of Europe. Direct influences can be seen in the cathedrals of Chartres and Senlis in particular. For twelve hundred years the former abbey church was the burial place of the kings of France, from the Merovingian Dagobert to the Bourbon Louis XVIII. The tombs are some of the most beautiful examples of medieval and Renaissance sculpture in France.

St-Eustache: The church on the edge of the area of les Halles is one of the most beautiful in Paris. It was begun in 1532 but not consecrated until a hundred years later. In both spirit and style it is still very much a Gothic church; the influence of Notre-Dame is very evident. The Renaissance decoration blends remarkably well with the Gothic architectural forms. Hector Berlioz and Franz Liszt gave the first performances of some of their works on the church's organ, and well-attended organ recitals still take place here.

St-Germain-l'Auxerrois, in the Place du Louvre, is certainly not the most beautiful but may be the most interesting church in Paris. It is a veritable museum of architectural styles, ranging over a period of five centuries. The lower part of the tower is Romanesque, the choir and main door Gothic, the porch and nave Late Gothic and the side doors Renaissance. The finest part of the church is probably the porch (1435–39), with its five arcades and three portals. Its bells are said to have been rung on August 24th 1572 as a signal for the Massacre of St Bartholomew to begin.

Secular architecture: The *Marais*, to which a whole tour has been devoted (see page 46), is no longer a secret. Hardly less attractive is the *Faubourg St-Germain* on the left bank of the Seine, which in the 18th c. saw the construc-

Architecture 21

The beautiful church of St-Eustache

tion of magnificent residences for the nobility. The largest and most renowned of these buildings is the *Palais Bourbon* (1722), which today is the seat of the National Assembly. The finest view of the Palais can be had from the Place de la Concorde and the bridge that crosses the Seine at this point. Of interest in the *Rue de Lille* are numbers 80 (Hôtel de Seignelay) and 78 (Hôtel de Beauharnais), the latter being the residence of the West German ambassador. Number 76 is the home of the Légion d'Honneur. At right angles to the Rue de Lille, the Rue de Bellechasse crosses the Boulevard St-Germain and leads to the *Rue de Grenelle*. Pay particular attention here to numbers 79 (Hôtel d'Estrées), 85 (Hôtel de Courteilles) and 138 to 140 (Hôtel de Noirmoutiers). In the *Rue de Varenne*, which runs parallel to the Rue de Grenelle, numbers 73 (Hôtel de Broglie), 78 (Hôtel de Villeroy) and 54 (Hôtel Matignon, official residence of the prime minister) are of particular interest. Since most of these mansions are now official buildings (ministries, embassies), it is unfortunately impossible to view them from the inside, except in special circumstances. However, the view from the outside is enough to make you realise that, in the final decades of the *ancien régime*, money, good taste and a cultivated lifestyle were by no means mutually exclusive.

Museums and exhibitions

For addresses see pages 70–73

There are more than fifty museums in Paris. And judged purely in terms of quantity, the Louvre alone is worth fifty more (see page 51). A selection appears below.

Musée des Arts Décoratifs: The collection includes antique furniture, carpets, enamelware, porcelain and faïence, and other decorative and ornamental objects which once graced castles and palaces. This beautiful collection gives a marvellous impression of the high quality and distinction of French arts and crafts, and an instructive overview of the historical development of styles, even using children's toys and book bindings as examples. Oriental works of art are also represented.

Musée Carnavalet: To many people, this collection may seem a mere hotchpotch, but that in itself can be attractive. The museum is housed in a Renaissance mansion and is the official museum of the city of Paris. It contains many objects that illustrate the history of the city from the time of Henri IV to the First World War, notably interesting exhibits from the period of the Revolution and many maps and views of the city. Several rooms are furnished with magnificent Louis XVI furniture. Finally, there are many items that have associations with Madame de Sévigné, whose residence this was for a time (see page 47).

The Grand Palais and Petit Palais, both built for the International Exhibition of 1900, and the Pont Alexandre III form an impressive architectural ensemble, even if the neo-Baroque forms of the *Belle Epoque* cannot always be judged beautiful. They give a good idea of the wealth that had been accumulated in *fin de siècle* France and which was to be put on display here. Both buildings are often the site of special exhibitions. The Petit Palais contains valuable collections of paintings donated to the city by private collectors, as well as the *Musée des Beaux-Arts de la Ville de Paris*, which has a collection of 19th c. French painting.

Musée de Cluny: The museum has one of the largest collections of medieval and Renaissance art and artefacts. Of particular interest are the Visigothic votive crowns, found in Spain, a gold altar from Basle (c. 1020) and the tapestries, for example the series of six 'millefleurs' tapestries known as 'La Dame à la Licorne' (Lady with the Unicorn). Since 1977, the twenty-one heads of the 'Kings of Israel', which once graced the west doorway of Notre-Dame, have been on display.

Musée d'Orsay: It was both courageous and imaginative to convert the old Gare d'Orsay, a building of the *Belle Epoque*, into a museum. The exterior of the magnificent building has been successfully preserved. Inside the vast station concourse, many visitors feel

Museums and exhibitions

Historic Musée de Cluny
Striking reflections of the illuminated Musée d'Orsay

overwhelmed by the awkward layout and the enormous number of exhibits. Moreover, it must be said that the period between 1848 and 1914 is also depicted through many second- and even third-class works, as well as through photography, film, design and furniture. The rooms containing Impressionist works from the much-loved *Jeu de Paume* are extremely crowded. An abundance of beautiful and valuable objects have been brought together in the Musée d'Orsay; however, this important museum, with its oppressive urban atmosphere, lacks calm and the opportunity for quiet reflection.

Centre Georges-Pompidou

Musée Picasso: Since 1986 the *Hôtel Salé*, a Baroque mansion in the Marais, has housed the largest Picasso collection in the world: more than 300 paintings, 158 sculptures, 88 ceramics and 1,500 drawings. The collection presents a fascinating insight into Picasso's versatility, and is magnificently housed in a setting that is both imposing and elegant.

Musée Jacquemart-André: An exquisite collection (paintings, furniture, carpets, etc.), with an emphasis on the 18th c. and the period of Louis XV.

Centre Georges-Pompidou: A cultural centre, conceived by former President Georges Pompidou and constructed between 1972 and 1977. The four principal cultural areas represented here are painting and the plastic arts, the printed word, industrial design and music. The *Musée National d'Art Moderne* occupies the largest space. Some of the classic modern works previously accommodated in the *Palais d'Art Moderne* were transferred to the permanent exhibition in the Pompidou Centre. Temporary exhibitions are also frequently held here. The terrace on the fifth floor affords fine views over central Paris. In 1983 a fountain with motifs inspired by Stravinsky was installed in front of the Pompidou Centre by the artists Niki de Saint-Phalle and Jean Tinguely.

Musée Rodin: On display here are all the works and collections that the famous sculptor Auguste Rodin (1850–1917) bequeathed to the French state, including such popular sculptures as *The Thinker* and *The Kiss*.

Food and drink

For addresses see pages 73–75

There are hundreds of North African, Chinese and Vietnamese restaurants in Paris, to say nothing of Argentinian steak-houses and German pubs. There is also an increasing number of self-service and fast-food restaurants, serving wretched food to tourists in a hurry. However, you would be well advised to frequent good French restaurants, for if you adopt this approach you can double the pleasure of your stay in Paris. There is no such thing as a Parisian cuisine: rather it is a meeting point for influences from all the French provinces, from Normandy to Périgord.

Bistros: These are small restaurants, usually simply furnished and family-run. They are generally very dependable. The menu is modest but sound, offering good value. Here you will see workers from the neighbourhood enjoying the food – always a good sign! In the course of time, many bistros have begun to cater for the tourist trade and now offer a *menu touristique* (starter, main course and dessert), with several choices per course, all for a fixed price that is very reasonable. A useful list of addresses is published under the title '*Paris – 700 restaurants accueillants et pas chers*' ('700 friendly, inexpensive restaurants in Paris'), which can be obtained free of charge from tourist information offices.

For more discerning tastes: For those looking for something more refined, the price will be somewhat higher. Fortunately, in France it is possible to eat very well not only in expensive-looking restaurants but also in apparently modest establishments. You just have to know where they are. The restaurants recommended on pages 73–75 have been thoroughly investigated by the author.

Those gourmets wishing to sample the heights of the gastronomic art should obtain a *Guide Michelin* or *Gault Millau* restaurant guide. In the establishments awarded one or more stars by these guides, and in those selected here, the diner can expect a sumptuous, imaginatively devised menu, with prominence given to either seasonal or particular regional specialities, together with attentive and knowledgeable service and, generally speaking, an excellent meal, for which adequate time, attention and money should be set aside. You should count on spending a fairly substantial sum per person. Don't worry about the drinks! The waiters will be glad to advise you. Many restaurants serve good table wines at reasonable prices, which also come in carafes and half-bottles.

Picnics: If you like to eat well but cannot always go to a restaurant, buy a baguette from a baker's shop, find the nearest delicatessen (*Comestibles, Charcuterie, Traiteur, Fromagerie*), buy a little pâté, some ripe cheese and a bottle of red wine, and have a cold meal in your room. The shopping can be a pleasure in itself and the food will

Food and drink

Paris offers excellent food...

...in the most sumptuous surroundings

certainly be better and cheaper than in any self-service restaurant.

An eldorado for gourmets: If you are an experienced gourmet, you will know the addresses of the world-famous palaces of gastronomy, *La Tour d'Argent, Lucas Carton, Jamin, Laurent, Lasserre* and *Taillevent*. And you will also have a sufficiently well-filled wallet, for you will know the high price of entry to these culinary paradises on earth.

If you are not an experienced gourmet, you would do better not to go to these restaurants. In all probability, you will not get your money's worth. For many people, the strain of doing everything correctly is just too restricting.

So where should one eat in Paris? The vast choice can often result in confusion.

Special recommendations: The *Jules Verne* (Métro: Ecole-Militaire), on the top platform of the Eiffel Tower, accessible via the south pillar. Light food, not cheap, but an unforgettable experience at night, high above the sea of lights of the big city.

The *Train bleu*, in the Gare de Lyon (Métro: Gare de Lyon). A special tip for epicures who would like to dine sumptuously in the magnificently decorated *Belle Epoque* rooms of the most beautiful station restaurant in the world.

High-class bistros: The following are some of the most beautiful restaurants in Paris, where you can not only eat very well, but also enjoy the nostalgic *Belle Epoque* atmosphere:
Benoît (20 Rue St-Martin, Métro: Rambuteau); *Brasserie Julien* (16 Rue du Faubourg-St-Denis, Métro: Strasbourg-St-Denis); *Pharamond* (Rue de la Grande-Truanderie, Métro: Les Halles).

The Train Bleu *restaurant*

The vocabulary of eating and drinking

Breakfast (*petit déjeuner*) can be obtained in your hotel, but that is boring! Go instead to the bar on the nearest corner. You do not have to breakfast in the austere French manner – espresso and cigarette – but can, for example, order a small or large cup of white coffee (*petit crème, grand crème*) and *croissants*, the somewhat larger rolls known as *brioches*, a chocolate-filled roll (*pain au chocolat*) or a slice of bread and butter (*tartine*).

Which restaurant? At midday and in the evening, you will first have to decide what kind of restaurant you want to eat in: a normal *restaurant*, a grillroom

Street café near the Arc de Triomphe

(*rôtisserie*), a simple eating-house (*bistro*), a pub or *brasserie*, or a self-service restaurant (*self-service, libre-service*). If you look at the menu hanging up outside, you will often see two options: a cheaper tourist menu (*menu touristique*) and one for the more discerning (*menu gastronomique*), which clearly does not apply to tourists!

Tipping: You should not overlook the somewhat ominous abbreviations next to the price. If the price includes the service charge, you will see s.c. (*service compris*); if it also includes a drink, you will see s.b.c. (*service et boisson compris*). If the service charge and drinks are extra, the words '*service et boisson en sus*' will appear on the menu. A separate cover charge (*couvert*) is nowadays the exception rather than the rule.

The menu (*la carte*) is the first thing you ask for in a restaurant. The simpler menus have three courses: a starter (*hors-d'oeuvre*), a main course and a dessert. As a rule, you can reckon that a fixed menu will be cheaper than eating à la carte.

Starters: Even in the most modest restaurants, there are always a few appetisers, or *hors-d'oeuvre*, on the menu: salami, ham, sardines in oil, olives, gherkins, a little salad. More refined appetisers include sophisticated pâtés and salads, *foie gras* (goose liver), artichokes, mussels, oysters and the like.

Main course: usually a meat course (*viande*). Some of the more common offerings are roast meats (*rôtis*), grills (*grillades*), poultry (*volaille*) or even game (*gibier*). You can order vegetables (*légumes*) or salad (*salade*) as an accompaniment.

An entrée, served before the main course, will also certainly be a feature of more elaborate menus. It may consist of fish (*poisson*) or eggs (*oeufs*). Soup is served only in the evenings; there is usually a choice between clear soups (*consommés*) and thickened soups (*potages*). In the relevant speciality restaurants, oysters (*huîtres*), seafood (*fruits de mer, moules, coquillages, crustacés*) and snails (*escargots*) will play a large part.

Dessert: the choice is usually between cheese (*fromage*), sweet puddings (*entremets*), pastries (*pâtisserie*), ice cream (*glace*) or fruit (*fruits*).

Wine list (*carte du vin*). Experienced wine-drinkers will probably have little difficulty with this item. In the first instance, they have only to choose between white wine (*vin blanc*), red wine (*vin rouge*) and rosé (*vin rosé*); then they allow themselves to be advised by the waiter. They will already be acquainted with most of the marks of origin: Alsace, Anjou, Beaujolais, Bordelais (Bordeaux), Bourgogne (Burgundy), Côtes-du-Rhône, Loire. Simple table wines (*vin ordinaire*) or local wines (*vins du pays*) are usually very satisfactory and not too costly, even in many of the more expensive restaurants, and are served already open, either in carafes or in jugs (*en pichet*).

On the appropriate occasions one can drink champagne, cider (*cidre*) or, if necessary, mineral water (*eau minérale*), which can be either carbonated (*gazeuse*) or still (*plate*). Surprisingly in a country of aperitif- and wine-drinkers, fruit juices (*jus de fruit*) and beer (*bière*) are becoming increasingly popular, particularly draught beer (*bière à la pression*).

To conclude your meal, you can order black coffee (*café noir*), white coffee (*café crème*), espresso (*café express*) or filter coffee (*café filtre*). Decaffeinated coffee (*café décaféiné*) is usually abbreviated to '*déca*'. And to accompany your coffee, order yourself a cognac, marc, cherry brandy (*kirsch*), plum brandy (*quetsch*) or white raspberry brandy (*framboise*). Cheers! (*Santé!*)

Historic places

For addresses see page 66

The Bastille, or bastion tower, built in the 14th c. as the Bastille St-Antoine, was the most hated building in 18th c. Paris. By that time it had become a sombre fortress prison, in whose dungeons famous men such as Voltaire and Mirabeau were incarcerated like common criminals. At the outbreak of the French Revolution the anger of the people was directed initially against this 'symbol of oppression'. On July 14th 1789 the Revolutionary mob stormed the Bastille (which also served as an arsenal), massacred its defenders and freed the prisoners. This day is still celebrated by the French as a national holiday. The following day, the Revolutionaries began to raze the Bastille to the ground. The only reminder of the building now is a line of bricks in the paving of the Place de la Bastille, marking the ground-plan. It can be seen most clearly from the platform of the July Column, which was erected to commemorate the insurgents killed in the revolution of July 1830. On the 200th anniversary of the storming of the Bastille, the new opera house was formally opened; its massive façade now dominates the square. As part of the anniversary celebrations, the whole district was given a face-lift and 'upgraded': art galleries, boutiques, etc. have taken the place of small craft workshops, particularly furniture-makers. Land prices and rent have rocketed.

Place de la Bastille

The Ecole Militaire

The Conciergerie

The Pont Alexandre III and the Dôme des Invalides

The Conciergerie, a fortress-like palace built in the 14th c., also served as a prison in the last years of the *ancien régime*. It was originally the residence of the 'Concierge', the head of the royal household. During the French Revolution it was the 'waiting room' for the guillotine, where 1,200 people awaited the departure of the tumbril for the Place de la Révolution, the present-day Place de la Concorde. The most celebrated prisoner held in the Conciergerie was the unfortunate Marie-Antoinette, wife of Louis XVI. Danton and Robespierre also awaited their deaths here. The Conciergerie is part of the huge complex of the Palais de Justice, as is the Sainte-Chapelle.

The Ecole Militaire was founded by Louis XV for the training of impoverished young noblemen as army officers. It stands at one end of the large-scale architectural ensemble formed by the Place du Trocadéro, Palais de Chaillot, Eiffel Tower and Champ de Mars. The once marshy land that now forms the *Champ de Mars* was laid out in the 18th c. as a parade ground. Many festivals were held here in the early years of the Revolution, including the Festival of the Federation on July 14th 1790, at which Lafayette took the oath to his country and the constitution in front of 300,000 people, and the Festival of the Higher Being, which was conceived by Robespierre as part of his substitute for Christianity. Two months after the first festival, held on June 8th 1794, Robespierre was himself led to the guillotine. The most famous and successful pupil of the Ecole Militaire, which is a superb example of French 18th c. architecture, was Napoleon Bonaparte. It was prophesied of the artillery lieutenant: 'He will go far if circumstances favour him.'

The Hôtel des Invalides was founded by Louis XIV and constructed between 1671 and 1676. In this large, self-contained complex, with living-quarters, mess and kitchen accommodation, hospital and church, 4,000 disabled soldiers (*invalides*) were to be cared for until the end of their days.

The Dôme des Invalides, also from the High Baroque period, is an impressive building dominated by a massive central dome, designed by the architect Hardouin-Mansart and inspired by Michelangelo's design for St Peter's in Rome. The exterior of the building is divided up by series of Doric and Corinthian columns. During the French Revolution it was renamed the Temple of Mars and became a sort of military shrine. It contains the graves of senior army officers and innumerable trophies from Napoleon's campaigns. In December 1840, Napoleon's mortal remains were brought back from his place of exile on St Helena and buried with full state honours in the Dôme des Invalides.

Opera, theatre and the concert hall

For addresses see pages 75, 76

Paris is a theatre city *par excellence*. For many people, however, the language barrier presents a virtually insurmountable obstacle to any enjoyment of stage performances, whether serious or light. Least problematic is an evening at the opera.

The opera scene: The main thing here is the music, and those who do not understand an opera libretto may sometimes even consider themselves fortunate! The Paris *Opéra* has always been renowned more for pomp and extravagance than for musical excellence: opera as spectacle rather than musical theatre. During the celebrations marking the bicentenary of the French Revolution in 1989, on the eve of Bastille Day, the Parisian opera scene was turned upside down by the ceremonial opening of the new Opera House, a gigantic temple of the Muses in the Place de la Bastille, for 2,800 spectators. The old *Opéra* now provides a glittering setting for no less splendid ballet productions and is indispensable for exclusive events. (See also page 43.)

The *Opéra-Comique*, now known as the *Salle Favart*, stages productions of popular operas, such as those of Rossini and Puccini, that are consciously aimed at a wide audience. The boundaries between such productions and the realm of light entertainment are somewhat fluid. Musicality and vivacity can always be expected from the sophisticated, imaginative productions of operettas and musicals staged at the Théâtre Musical de Paris (previously known as the *Théâtre du Châtelet*), which is by no means the only theatre of its kind.

In the theatre world, the *Comédie-Française*, next to the Palais Royal, occupies an undisputed special position. This theatre presents traditional productions of the great French classics by Racine, Corneille, Molière and a few others. An imperfect grasp of the French language should not under any circumstances prevent dedicated theatregoers from attending one of these performances. With the aid of a text, it should be possible to follow the action without too much difficulty, particularly since the spoken word is accompanied on stage by dramatic gestures.

At the *Odéon-Théâtre de France*, a sort of branch of the Comédie-Française, the productions are predominantly of works by modern dramatists. This makes for greater difficulties in understanding, especially if one has problems appreciating modern works in one's own language!

Commercial theatres: In addition to the subsidised theatres, there are around 100 commercial theatres – their lifespan is very variable – catering for all tastes. If you so wished, it would be possible to see a different play every night for a month in Paris. The established, commercially very successful

The Opéra

theatres, such as the *Arts-Hébertot*, the *Athenée-Louis-Jouvet*, the *Comédie des Champs-Elysées* and the *Studio des Champs-Elysées*, can depend on an appreciative core of support. As you would expect, the experimental theatres are not in the commercial and tourist centres, but in the outlying districts. The TEP (*Théâtre de l'Est Parisien*), for example, is in the 20th arrondissement and puts on plays by Ionesco, Beckett and Brecht, among others; its motto is 'culture for the workers, not for the educated middle classes'. There are other experimental, literary theatres in the suburbs, such as the *Cartoucherie* in a former powder mill in Vincennes, which has become famous for the productions of Ariane Mnouchkine, and the *Théâtre des Amandiers de Nanterre* in the student town of Nanterre, whose artistic profile has been raised by Patrice Chéreau. Those not wishing to go so far afield can see interesting plays and thought-provoking productions at the *Théâtre de Chaillot* (at Trocadéro) or at the *Théâtre Renaud-Barrault* (in the Avenue F.D. Roosevelt).

The cafés-théâtres, or theatre workshops, represent a particular form of theatre in Paris. They are small, and present all kinds of experimental, avant-garde performances. Those without good French will be more or less lost in these establishments, even if many points are conveyed through mime. The most successful cafés-théâtres at the moment include *Au Bec Fin*, *Café d'Edgar* and *Aux blancs Manteaux*.

The concert programme in Paris is remarkably crowded and of exceptional quality. An evening performance of religious music at *Notre-Dame Cathedral* and a Sunday afternoon organ concert at *St-Eustache* or *St-Séverin* are musical experiences of a kind that only Paris can offer.

Paris by night

For addresses see pages 76, 77

What an experience! The city is bursting at the seams with vitality. The centres of nightlife — along the Champs-Elysées, around the Opéra, in the Latin Quarter, St-Germain-des-Prés, Montparnasse and Montmartre, and around the Place de la Bastille — are filled with crowds of people out to have a good time. Glittering neon advertisements turn night into day, the traffic roars continuously and nobody seems to be thinking of going to bed.

For night-owls, nightlife in Paris means just that: in many cinemas the last showing does not start until after midnight, opera- and theatregoers have a wide choice of restaurants for a meal after the performance, and everywhere there are bars, nightclubs and disco-

A traditional Parisian structure — advertising a traditional Parisian show!

thèques which do not close until dawn. Everybody can take part in this 'official' nightlife. If the company is good, a night in Paris will never be too long. There is always so much happening that it is no exaggeration to call Paris the most entertaining city in the world.

Things are more difficult for the tourist wishing to experience Parisian nightlife in the more specialised sense. This kind of nightlife, which is aimed principally at foreign tourists, is either expensive or seedy – as it is everywhere in the world.

Glittering revues: It is an expensive business to see a show at one of the large, internationally renowned variety theatres, with their traditional revues, more or less luxurious surroundings, pretty, scantily clad girls, vitality and imagination.

If dinner is included in the programme (*Dîner-Spectacle*), it will be as well to reckon on spending a substantial sum of money. A standing-place at the bar will be cheaper, but you will not be able to see as well what is happening on stage, and that is presumably what you

Spectacular lights on the Eiffel Tower

Paris by night

The internationally famous Moulin Rouge

are going for. In the established variety theatres, you can be sure that the show will not be a complete washout. The theatre will be well appointed, the shows are often witty and stylish, and the girls are of course good to look at, so the erotic content is never in short supply. You will thus be offered something for your money. However, it is unlikely that you will have a truly memorable evening, particularly if you go on one of the coach trips that claim to show 'Paris by night'. In a group of predominantly elderly tourists, you will lose any contact you may possibly have had with so-called Parisian life. You should not waste either time or money on such futile excursions!

Nightclubs and discos are two a penny; most have only a short life. Fame can be very ephemeral indeed, particularly if they have the dubious good fortune to become the 'in' place for a few months. As soon as word gets round outside the 'happy few' who like to hang around together, this narrow, select circle moves on to a new, undiscovered venue, where anonymous unknowns or those who are not fashionably dressed (or fashionably accompanied) will find it impossible to get past the door. Those willing to take the risk may make some interesting discoveries in the area behind the *Place de la Bastille*, which became ultra-fashionable during the bicentenary year of 1989. The *Rue de Lappe*, for example, which even in the 1930s had an unfortunate reputation, is returning to its old ways.

Prostitution in its seediest forms flourishes on the boulevard below Montmartre and in the small side-streets between Place Clichy and Place Pigalle – bad pornographic movies, cheap prostitution, a little crime for provincial bumpkins and foreign tourists. The same is true of the Rue St-Denis and its side-streets. Tourists should at least be aware of the reputations of such areas.

Haute couture and fashion

For addresses see pages 77, 78

Haute couture is very much alive in Paris; no doubt about that. Yet this has not entirely protected the established fashion capital of the world from younger competitors. In London, Rome and even New York, it was suddenly decided that the dictators on the Seine should no longer be allowed to rule the fashion world. And it is probable that the French couturiers will never win back their unique position.

Nevertheless, Paris will remain the home of haute couture. No other city has its special flair, which can be neither exported nor imitated, however advanced the tailors and however capable the business people in other cities. And where, except in Paris, are there so many women who know how to wear fashionable clothes?

There are two locations where the city's incomparably fashionable ambience becomes an almost tangible reality.

Champs-Elysées: One of these centres of fashion is the triangle of streets made up of the Champs-Elysées, the *Avenue Montaigne* and the *Avenue George V*, in which the fashion houses of Christian Dior, Balenciaga, Pierre Balmain, Courrèges and Givenchy, among others, have their headquarters. These are quiet, elegant streets with palatial houses, behind whose shuttered façades creative ideas for the coming collections are born and tested. Just to stand in front of those lofty entrance doors will send a slight shiver of reverence down the spine.

Twice a year, however, in February and August, the couturiers step into the limelight, for the solemn ritual of presenting the collections which determine the coming season's fashions. Within a reasonable period after the opening, ordinary mortals, even tourists, can view the collections, provided they telephone beforehand. Nobody is expected to buy anything on the spot, which is as it should be.

Rue du Faubourg St-Honoré: The other side of the fashion capital is most

Epitomising haute couture – the house of Christian Dior

Haute couture and fashion

A spring fashion show

evident in the Rue du Faubourg St-Honoré. While the Champs-Elysées has succumbed to the excesses of mass tourism, the Rue du Faubourg St-Honoré, which has to some extent taken its place, is perhaps still the most Parisian and thus the most elegant shopping street in the world. However, it is facing increasing competition from the *Avenue Montaigne*. Both streets are lined with shops in whose windows fashion goods are lovingly and temptingly displayed, with that flair for luxury that can make the heart beat faster. The names to be found here include Gucci, Lanvin, Ted Lapidus, Daniel Hechter, Charles Jourdan, Lancôme, Alexandre, Pierre Cardin, Chanel, Vuitton, Bulgari, Harry Winston, Roger & Gallet and Hermès, which is famous not only for its handbags, belts and scarves, but also for the most beautiful window displays in the whole of Paris.

Politicians in the Fashion Mile:

You can wander for hours through these enticing streets, even if you do not overestimate the importance of elegance and taste in life. And suddenly, you notice something else: in the midst of this remarkable accumulation of haute couture, fur and leather goods, and perfume and cosmetics salons in the Rue du Faubourg St-Honoré lives not only the British ambassador but also, in the historic Palais de l'Elysée, the president of France. Whoever the current incumbent may be, he cannot be in any doubt about one thing at least, namely the extraordinary role that luxury, beauty and elegance play in his country's capital city!

Shopping

For addresses see pages 78–81

If you have a liking for fashionable elegance or antiques, luxury or cheap odds and ends, in Paris you can satisfy all your wishes, and it is easier here than anywhere else in the world to spend a fortune in an innocent afternoon's shopping. Here are a few suggestions:

Clothes: If you know what you want to buy (leaving high fashion to one side for the time being), you are recommended to visit the large department stores. The variety is inexhaustible. However, you should not expect to find any great bargains. Even elegant Parisian ladies come here to buy a pair of smart shoes or a day dress. Many a woman looks forward to her next trip to Paris above all for the chance to rummage around again in *Printemps* or *Samaritaine*.

Jewellery: The finest and most expensive jewellers — Cartier, Mauboussin,

Printemps *department store*

Flea-market at Clignancourt

Boucheron, Van Cleef & Arpels — are to be found around the *Place Vendôme*. If you walk down the *Rue St-Honoré* in the direction of the Rue Royale, in which, incidentally, the main Christofle shop is located, you will find lovely old and new silver items on sale at relatively reasonable prices.

Porcelain and glass: The paradise for shoppers looking for the finest French tableware is in the aptly named *Rue du Paradis*, near the Gare de l'Est, not a particularly elegant district. But don't let that put you off, for here you will find a huge selection of porcelain and earthenware, and glass and crystal tableware and ornaments.

Antiques: There is a great amount of antique furniture on sale in France. French cabinet-makers are remarkably adept at conjuring up, say, two old tables out of one old chair. So if you are not an expert, be careful. For this reason, it is very difficult to make reliable recommendations. If you buy any large items, you should insist on a certificate of origin.

Many antique-shops are concentrated around the *Rue du Faubourg St-Honoré*, in the *Rue Lafitte* and, on the Left Bank, between the *Rue de Seine* and the *Rue des Saints-Pères*.

Antiquarian books: Do not expect too much of the *bouquinistes* along the Seine. They add colour to the scene, but have little of interest in their stock. The most promising shops are in the district between the *Boulevard St-Michel*, the *Boulevard St-Germain* and the *Seine*.

Prints will be found in the same district as that recommended for antiquarian books, i.e. around the *Ecole des Beaux-Arts*, the art school. In the *Rue Jacob, Rue Bonaparte, Rue St-Benoît* and *Rue Visconti*, artists of every rank wait for you to discover them – for a price! Take a chance with a print or two!

Delicatessens: There are of course exquisite delicatessens in all districts of Paris, even the most modest. However, the holy of holies for gourmets is the *Place de la Madeleine*. And there is no cheaper pleasure than to feast one's eyes on all the choice delicacies, of which after all only a tiny fraction can be consumed. *Maison de la Truffe:* the specialist shop for truffles and Strasbourg pâté de foie gras; *Hédiard:* for unusual specialities from abroad; *Fauchon:* one of the largest delicatessens in the world; *Tanrade:* the most refined sweet creations; *Creplet-Brussol:* lord of hundreds of varieties of cheese. An even greater cheese artist is the legendary *Androuet* (at 41 Rue Amsterdam, close to the Gare St-Lazare), who also runs a cheese restaurant. The third star in the Parisian cheese universe is *La Ferme St-Hubert*, at 21 Rue Vignon, with an endless array of special varieties.

A Paris bakery

Book and print stalls by the Seine

Souvenir-hunting

Suggested tours of the city

The extravagant ornamentation of Garnier's Opéra

Around the Place de l'Opéra

A world city usually has several rival centres. Paris is no exception. It is a matter for debate where the heart of the city really lies: on the Île de la Cité, in the Latin Quarter, or perhaps around the *Place de l'Opéra*? Whatever the answer may be, you should make a conscious effort to absorb the atmosphere of this square. Position yourself on the traffic island in the middle, and calmly look around you (although with the roar of traffic coming from all sides, any calm there may be will be strictly figurative!). From here, you will obtain a superb impression of the very special atmosphere that still prevails in Paris.

Now begin with the *Opéra*, which has given its name both to the square and to the surrounding district. Since 1989 operas have been performed in the new opera house in the Place de la Bastille. The grandiose old building, designed by Charles Garnier and begun in 1862, is today considered excessively lavish in its decoration. Yet its ostentatious façade makes it a brilliantly appropriate monument to the Second Empire. Similarly, the rows of houses that line the boulevards around the Opéra reflect the spirit of the age of Napoleon III. With their mixture of ostentation and magnanimity, the upper-middle classes spared no expense when it came to flaunting their own status and wealth. Anyone who had money was a gentleman, and anyone who wanted to be a gentleman had to have money. It was to this dubious philosophy of life that the Paris of that period owed its undisputed position as the centre of the civilised world – a position it held until the outbreak of the First World War – as well as its remarkable unity of planning and architecture. For all that, the *grands boulevards*, with their elegant terraces, high windows, filigree balcony-railings and decorative sculpture, were a favourite subject of the Impressionist painters (see page 23).

Haussmann's boulevards

Take a stroll now through the boulevards around the Opéra. Leave the *Avenue de l'Opéra* behind on your right. With its offices of the kind to be found in all cities, particularly those of airlines and travel agencies, it holds little attraction for the sightseer. Turn instead into the *Boulevard des Capucines*, which becomes the *Boulevard des Italiens*. Here there are many fine shops, a number of large first-run cinemas, newspaper kiosks, flower stalls and the delightful shade of the maple trees and acacias – it is a marvel that they can still flourish here. At the end of the Boulevard des Italiens, turn left into the *Boulevard Haussmann*. It is named after Baron Georges Eugène Haussmann (d. 1891) who, during the reign of Napoleon III, laid out the *grands boulevards* around the Opéra and, as a result of his logical yet ruthless city planning, turned Paris into a 'modern' metropolis.

Behind the Opéra are two famous department stores, *Galeries Lafayette* and *Magasin au Printemps* (see page 78). Anyone interested in old railway stations should make a detour to the *Gare St-Lazare*, where the trains for Normandy depart. Cross the Rue Tronchet to the *Place de la Madeleine* and the church of *Ste-Marie-Madeleine*. Over a period of seventy years it was proposed that this building should be a church, parliament, stock exchange, library, temple to the glory of the Grande Armée, and station, until it was finally consecrated as a church in 1842. Its external appearance is that of a Greek temple. It is enough to view the church from the outside. However, you should not miss the magnificent view from its steps down the Rue Royale and over the Place de la Concorde to the Palais Bourbon and the Dôme des Invalides.

Parisian elegance

The *Rue Royale* is one of the most elegant streets in Paris. And at no. 3, shortly before the Place de la Concorde, is the restaurant that for many is the finest in the world: *Maxim's*. Not exactly the place for a quick snack. But even if you were willing to shell out a few hundred francs for a dinner for two it would not be advisable. True, the cooking is still very good. But it is probably

Panorama of the city and the Seine

only oil sheikhs, European aristocrats and their like who will feel comfortable at Maxim's.

Cast a sidelong glance at the *Place de la Concorde*, but save it up for another time (see page 49) and go back to the *Rue St-Honoré*, into which you turn right. (To the left it leads into the *Rue du Faubourg St-Honoré*; see page 38.) This is also an elegant street, full of luxury and refinement, as is the *Rue de Castiglione*, which leads to the *Place Vendôme*. The architectural unity of this famous square makes it a magnificent display of royal splendour, and a fitting monument to the greatest period of French history. It was built for Louis XIV; the architect was Hardouin-Mansart and the works were supervised by Louvois, chief superintendent of the royal buildings. The *Vendôme Column*, 44 m in height and designed in the style of Trajan's Column in Rome, was commissioned by Napoleon I and constructed from the metal of 1,200 cannons captured at the Battle of Austerlitz. Encircling the column is a spiral band of bas-reliefs depicting scenes from the battle. The column is surmounted by a statue of Napoleon.

Place Vendôme is perhaps an even more distinguished address than the Rue Royale. Occupants of the square include the *Ritz*, the luxury hotel rich in tradition, some of the most exclusive private banks from the Old and New Worlds and the most expensive jewellers. Equally exclusive is the adjoining *Rue de la Paix*, which leads back to the *Place de l'Opéra*.

Nostalgia in the Café de la Paix

Naturally you will want to finish your tour of the Opéra district at the legendary *Café de la Paix*. Most tourists stay outside on the terrace, whereas regular customers sit inside where, in addition to their coffee or aperitif, they can enjoy the refined calm and splendid original *fin de siècle* décor. The café, renovated in 1976, is listed as a historic monument.

The Vendôme Column

The Marais

The Marais, so called from the marshy land (*marais* = marsh) drained by monks in the Middle Ages, lies in the east of the city. From the 16th to the 18th c. it was a fashionable residential district for the aristocracy. After the Revolution, the area went into decline. It was not until 1962, on the initiative of de Gaulle's Minister of Culture, André Malraux, that the work of restoration began, and much of the area's valuable architectural and cultural heritage has now been rescued.

The Marais lies a little apart from the most famous tourist attractions, and one has to make it a specific destination. A little patience and a feeling for history are also required. The district's architectural treasures, which account for its charm, are not always immediately apparent in their generally unassuming surroundings.

The starting point for the tour is the *Hôtel de Ville* (Town Hall) Métro station. Incidentally, this town hall is not as old as it looks; its predecessor was burnt down by the Communards in 1871, and this replacement, in the style of the French Renaissance, was erected between 1874 and 1884. Cross over the Rue de Rivoli and walk down the Rue des Archives to the *Rue des Francs-Bourgeois*, which provides a point of reference for all visitors to the Marais who get lost in the maze of narrow streets. In and near the Rue des Francs-Bourgeois are three of the main places of interest in the Marais: the *Hôtel de Soubise*, the *Hôtel Carnavalet* and the *Place des Vosges*.

Baroque mansions

Most of the rectangular area bounded by the *Rue des Archives, Rue des*

Francs-Bourgeois, *Rue Vieille-du-Temple* and *Rue des 4 Fils* is occupied by the Hôtel de Soubise and the Hôtel de Rohan, both of which house the French National Archives. The *Hôtel de Soubise* is a city mansion built on an extravagant scale in the first half of the 18th c. Leading artists of the time worked on the interior decoration. (On the first floor is a 'Museum of the History of France'.) The *Hôtel de Rohan*, the entrance to which is in the Rue Vieille-du-Temple, is more modest in appearance, but also has several magnificent rooms. Opposite the entrance to the Hôtel de Soubise is a tower that once formed part of the city fortifications built by Philippe II.

Walk past the *Hôtels d'Almeyras* (no. 30) and *de Sandreville* (no. 26), which contains a museum of the Marais, to the *Hôtel de Lamoignon* (entrance in the Rue Pavée). The mansion was built in 1585 for an illegitimate daughter of Henri II. It now houses the Bibliothèque Historique de la Ville de Paris, whose reading room, with its carefully restored wooden-beamed ceiling, is a successful example of the rehabilitation of the Marais.

Opposite the Hôtel de Lamoignon are the walls of the *Hôtel Carnavalet* (entrance in the Rue de Sévigné). The buildings round the first courtyard date from the period around 1550, and the façade from 1655. The buildings surrounding the three inner gardens were built in the 19th c. The museum housed in the Hôtel (see page 22) illustrates the history of Paris from the 16th to the 19th c.; it also contains items associated with Madame de Sévigné (the famous letter-writer, who lived here from 1677 to 1696), and boasts a magnificent collection of Louis Quinze and Louis Seize furniture.

Left: The Hôtel de Ville

Rue du Parc Royal

If you follow the *Rue de Sévigné*, you will come to the *Rue du Parc Royal*. Opposite the orangery in the *Square Léopold-Achille* stand four old city mansions (nos. 4, 8, 10 and 12) which individually are not great pieces of architecture, but when viewed as a whole give a good impression of what the Marais used to look like. If you are interested in old buildings and their construction, you can make some worthwhile discoveries here.

Walk along the Rue du Parc Royal towards the Hôtel de Rohan, i.e. towards the city, as far as the Place de Thorigny, and turn right into the *Rue de Thorigny*. At no. 5 is the *Hôtel Salé*, now the Picasso Museum (see page 24).

Place des Vosges

Now walk back to the *Rue des Francs-Bourgeois*, which leads to the Place des Vosges. This is the oldest and perhaps the most beautiful large square in Paris. It dates back to the time of Henri IV, whose idea it was to turn what was then a deserted area into an elegant residential district. The large quadrangle is surrounded by thirty-six town residences built in the same imposing style, which were totally renovated for the bicentenary of the Revolution in 1989. The atmosphere is refined, charming and at the same time almost intimate. During the French Revolution, the Place Royale was renamed the Place des Vosges, after the department that was most punctual in delivering its taxes! Anyone interested in the writer Victor Hugo will find a museum in his former dwelling at no. 6. Also worthy of note is the *Hôtel de Béthune-Sully*, which is now occupied by offices of the Monuments Historiques, where information on the historic monuments of Paris can be obtained (62 Rue St-Antoine).

Suggested tours of the city

The triumphal way: Louvre – Tuileries – Concorde – Champs-Elysées – Place de l'Etoile (Charles-de-Gaulle)

In Paris, the capital city of a powerful state, pomp and ceremony have always played an important role. Glittering self-advertisement has always been a part of politics – under the presidency of de Gaulle as under the monarchy of Louis XIV. Indeed the French monarchy and the two Napoleonic empires bequeathed the Republic a magnificent stage for its state ceremonies, extending from the Louvre to the Place de l'Etoile. That is quite a distance for the conscientious tourist who wants to cover the whole route. The *Champs-Elysées*, for example, were laid out not for pedestrians but for horse-drawn carriages and gentlemen on horseback. So what is the answer? Public transport offers no solution. Perhaps you have your own car with you. But then you will have to concentrate on the traffic, which is particularly chaotic here, and you will see nothing. Instead go to the *Place du Louvre* (Métro: Louvre) and take a taxi from the taxi-rank there. Arrange with the driver that he should take you – slowly! – to the *Place de l'Etoile* and back. Ask him to drive once round the *Place du Carrousel* and also round the *Place de la Concorde*. The drive will take about half an hour.

The area around the Louvre

Opposite the taxi-rank is the oldest part of the *Palais du Louvre*, which is open to visitors just as the *Louvre Museum* is. The car will turn into the *Rue de Rivoli* and drive along the north front of the Louvre. On the right is the *Place du Palais Royal*, and in the background the Palais Royal, now the seat of the Council of State. On the left, a great archway leads into the *Place du Carrousel*, from the middle of which there is a magnificent view up to the Arc de Triomphe and also into the inner courtyard of the

Louvre, with the intensely controversial glass pyramid. The smaller *Arc de Triomphe du Carrousel* is a copy of the Triumphal Arch of Septimius Severus in Rome and was built between 1806 and 1808 to commemorate Napoleon's victories.

You will now return to the Rue de Rivoli and drive along the *Jardin des Tuileries*, a park laid out in typical 17th c. French style, in which nature is subordinated to the laws of geometry and symmetry. After your visit to the Louvre, you can go for a walk here, if you still have the energy, and enjoy the fine views.

Place de la Concorde

On your right, glance quickly down the Rue Royale to the *Madeleine* (see page 44). For many, the Place de la Concorde is one of the most beautiful squares in the world; it is certainly one of the busiest. In the centre rises the Obelisk of Luxor, an ancient monolith from Thebes in upper Egypt, 23 m high and dating from the 13th c. BC. Two fountains and eight statues personifying the great provincial capitals of France complete the artistic creations in the square. It is at its most beautiful when the warm light of its lamps mingles with that of the setting sun. At that time of day, it is difficult to imagine that, in the bloodiest years of the French Revolution, the guillotine

Place de la Concorde

The Arc de Triomphe du Carrousel – in the Place du Carrousel

Left: The Jardin des Tuileries

The lively Champs-Elysées

stood here; among its victims were Marie-Antoinette, Danton and Robespierre. The Palais Bourbon, today the seat of the French National Assembly, can be seen on the other side of the river.

Champs-Elysées

The start of this magnificent avenue is marked by two equestrian statues, masterpieces of French Baroque. The Champs-Elysées ('Elysian Fields') were laid out as early as the beginning of the 18th c., but it was not until the Second Empire that they became a fashionable promenade, renowned throughout the world. They were a meeting place for respectable society and the *demi-monde*, for gentlemen and cocottes. The avenue was lined with countless restaurants, cafés and places of entertainment.

The lower part of the Champs-Elysées, up to the *Rond-Point*, goes through a park with beautiful old chestnut-trees, children's playgrounds and the exclusive restaurant *Ledoyen*. At the *Place Clemenceau* the massive bulk of the *Grand Palais*, with its statues of horse-drawn chariots dripping with gold, becomes visible on the left; like the *Petit Palais* opposite, it was built for the International Exhibition of 1900. The scale and neo-Baroque ostentation of both the Grand and Petit Palais make them characteristic examples of their period, when evidently nothing was too extravagant (see page 22).

The upper section of the Champs-Elysées has lost much of its atmosphere. The broad avenue is flanked by very ordinary buildings, which accommodate banks, car showrooms, airline offices and department stores. Yet even if this section is no longer elegant, the Champs-Elysées has remained France's ceremonial avenue. This is the route of great state processions, the place where crowds gather when the president of the Republic welcomes foreign guests of honour – and the setting for the most fervent demonstrations.

Place Charles-de-Gaulle

The Champs-Elysées ends in the grandiose splendour of the *Place de l'Etoile*,

Suggested tours of the city

The Arc de Triomphe

officially renamed Place Charles-de-Gaulle after de Gaulle's death. It lies at the point where twelve avenues converge, disgorging their traffic into the Place. The largest of these, after the Champs-Elysées, is the *Avenue de la Grande Armée*, which extends the road that begins at the Louvre as far as the modern business and residential suburb of *La Défense*, a distance of 2½ miles. The *Arc de Triomphe* stands in the centre of the Place; it was begun in 1806 on the order of Napoleon as a monument to the French army and, after many interruptions, was completed in 1836. It is at its most impressive when viewed from a distance. Seen from the Tuileries, perhaps in mist or at dusk, it looms like a monster.

On the summit is a viewing platform, accessible by lift or stairs, commanding panoramic, and instructive, views of Paris. The opportunity should not be missed. You will see more in the morning or late afternoon than around midday.

Depending on whether you want to visit the whole palace or just the museum, return now to the *Place du Louvre* or to the pyramid, the main entrance to the museum.

Louvre
The palace

In 1527 François I began building a modern palace on the site of an old fortress (whose foundation walls have recently been excavated and can now be seen from the museum). From then onwards, the Louvre was subject to over 300 years of conversion, extension and rebuilding. Only under Napoleon III was the palace to achieve its definitive shape. It is all the more remarkable, therefore, that the whole ensemble appears so unified. However, the Louvre is not exactly rich in brilliant architectural achievements. The east façade of the Old Louvre with its magnificent colonnades, overlooking the Place du Louvre, is probably the work of the architect Claude Perrault and was built between 1667 and 1673. The old inner courtyard, the *Cour Carrée*, particularly the south-west section designed during the reign of François I, creates a truly beautiful impression of spaciousness. It is one of the masterpieces of French Renaissance architecture. Even the Baroque Pavillon de l'Horloge of 1624 fits in very harmoniously. Unless you are a dedicated palace enthusiast, you can disregard the history of the building of the various sections. The Louvre impresses simply through its size and unity.

The museum

Love and the Louvre are the two great misconceptions to which inexperienced visitors traditionally fall prey in Paris. They expect too much of the former, and too little of the latter. The Louvre is possibly (nobody knows exactly) the

The Louvre

largest museum in the world; its catalogues list more than 400,000 works of art. But what does this actually mean? In effect the Louvre consists of six different museums: (1) Egyptian antiquities; (2) Greek and Roman antiquities; (3) Oriental antiquities; (4) European sculpture; (5) European painting and drawing; (6) objets d'art and furniture; and this is to say nothing of branches such as the Musée de Cluny, the ceramic collection at Sèvres and the Musée d'Orsay. Anyone seriously interested in the subject could easily spend months in each section. It makes absolutely no sense to rush through the Louvre in one or two hours, for that just means racing through endless galleries and seeing nothing (see page 70).

The Louvre pyramid

The pyramid

The glass pyramid, opened in 1989 as part of the bicentenary celebrations of the French Revolution, is rather like the tip of an iceberg: it is the highly conspicuous outward sign of a total reorganisation of what is probably the largest museum in the world, a process likely to stretch well into the 1990s. This reorganisation has the following three aims: to put more items on display, to make room for more visitors, and to adapt the museum to the requirements of the next millennium! After the costly reorganisation process is completed, visitors who now have to put up with building-work and irritating closures will no longer be presented with collections of rubble, but will find clarity, information and stimulation at various levels, as well as every possible comfort.

The islands in the Seine

The *Île de la Cité* is the germ cell of the city of Paris. Long before the Romans, it was the site of a Celtic settlement: around 200 BC a Gallic tribe called the Parisii founded the town of Lutuhezi, meaning 'surrounded by water'. During the Roman period an altar to Jupiter stood on the island, the city was renamed Lutetia Parisiorum, and the important trading route from Soissons to Orléans followed the course of the present-day *Rue de la Cité*. Clovis I, who had united the kingdom of the Franks, is said to have died in the royal palace of the Merovingians, which stood on the site of the Palais de Justice. The crypt under Notre-Dame, open since 1980, amplifies the picture of historical Paris. Among the exhibits is a central-heating system from Roman times.

However, a little imagination is required to detect the heartbeat of historical Paris on the Île de la Cité. Practically everything that had not been destroyed by the ravages of time had, by the 19th c. at the latest, been knocked down or reconstructed. Massive building complexes such as the Palais de Justice, the Préfecture de Police and the hospital of Hôtel-Dieu were erected, and wide avenues were laid out. However, the island has of course retained its unique position in the heart of the city, and this can best be appreciated from the *quais* on the Left Bank. The architectural wonders of Notre-Dame and the Sainte-Chapelle have also been preserved.

Notre-Dame – nightfall

Churches on the Île de la Cité

Even the cathedral of *Notre-Dame-de-Paris* has experienced bad times over the centuries. Senseless destruction and unsympathetic restoration have added to the damage. However, it is still what it has always been: the national cathedral of France. It marks the final break between Early Gothic architecture and the preceding Romanesque tradition. Art historians can follow the gradual progress of the new style that developed as the cathedral was being built between 1163 and 1345. Yet the measured, harmonious proportions of the building, both inside and out, can be perceived and admired even without detailed knowledge. Look at the façade with its doorways, the Kings' Gallery and the magnificent rose window, the open arcade and the two squat towers: a marvellous balance of vertical and horizontal elements! Walk round the cathedral, immerse yourself in the fantastical yet precisely constructed maze of the abutment system, with its flying buttresses and pinnacles, and the famous gargoyles. And do not overlook the two magnificent doorways in the transept: the cloister door to the north, and the south door with the story of St Stephen depicted in the tympanum, with the filigree rose windows above.

The interior has a less striking effect. The subdued light does not show the height and breadth of the space to its best advantage, and as a result it appears almost oppressive and gloomy. And yet the elevation of the walls in the nave is a masterpiece of Early Gothic architecture, and the unity of the ground-plan can be appreciated as a work of art in itself.

The *Sainte-Chapelle* glitters like a precious gem in a secluded corner in one of the inner courtyards of the vast Palais de Justice, on the site of which stood the first royal palace in Paris. It was built in only three years, between 1245 and 1248, and marks the culmination of French High Gothic. Louis IX (St Louis) had it built as a shrine for the relics he had acquired at great cost in the East, including a branch from the Crown of Thorns and a fragment of the True Cross. Four queens were crowned here. The church consists in fact of two superimposed chapels; the lower one, for servants and retainers, has a massive vaulted roof, while in the upper one, reserved for the royal family and court, the principles of the Gothic style are taken to their logical conclusion. It has virtually no walls, only narrow buttresses which come together in the high vaulting; in between them are sublime stained-glass windows depicting more than 1,000 biblical scenes. The light that floods in through the windows transfigures the space and dissolves the earthly material that defines it – the architectural expression of the Gothic mysticism of light.

A walk round the Île de la Cité

It is commonplace to liken the shape of the Île de la Cité to that of a ship's hull. The 'prow' is the spit of land projecting into the Seine to the west of the Pont Neuf, which was constructed in 1604 and is, despite its name, the oldest bridge in Paris. The *Square du Vert Galant* on this western extremity of the island – with a monument to Henri IV – is a delightful spot, ideal for relaxing and daydreaming. The 'stern' of the ship, the *Square de l'Île-de-France* behind Notre-Dame, is almost equally delightful. At its furthest extremity, a flight of steps leads down to the impressive memorial to the 200,000 Frenchmen deported to German concentration camps (*Mémorial de la Déportation*). A bridge leads to the Île St-Louis opposite.

Île St-Louis

Anyone seeking respite from the rigours of sightseeing on the Île de la Cité and a chance to experience a little more atmosphere should find an hour or so for a walk on the Île St-Louis. Just a few steps over the bridge and you are in another world. The smaller of the two islands was not made habitable until the 17th c., when it became a popular residential district for the aristocracy and wealthy middle classes. Outwardly, little seems to have changed since that time. The remarkably uniform architecture has a private, almost intimate character, although there are several extremely imposing mansions, such as the *Hôtel de Lauzun* and the *Hôtel Lambert*, both on the *Quai d'Anjou*. The richly decorated church of *St-Louis-en-l'Île* dates from the period of transition from Baroque to Rococo.

This delightful area is also one of the most expensive residential districts in the city. The nice thing about it is that this is by no means obvious from the appearance of the houses. Georges Pompidou lived and died as president of the French Republic on the *Quai de Béthune*. Before you leave the island, you can fortify yourself in the *Brasserie de l'Île St-Louis* with a substantial casserole and draught Alsace beer. And the bar is a meeting place for all sorts of interesting people.

The Latin Quarter and St-Germain-des-Prés

The *Quartier Latin* was once the Roman residential district, and thus is the oldest part of Paris after the Île de la Cité. However, it is called the Latin Quarter not because it was inhabited by the Romans in Caesar's time, but rather because until 1789 Latin was spoken at the university – teachers and pupils alike used Latin even as the language of everyday life. Today this is the centre of intellectual and academic life in France. But academic life here is somewhat different from what you may imagine, a characteristic which has its roots in the historical development of the area.

The first institutions of learning, founded during the age of Charlemagne, were dominated by the clergy on the Île de la Cité. It was not until the 12th c. that intellectuals were able to free themselves from the ecclesiastical establishment and move to the monasteries on the Mont Ste-Geneviève (Abelard was one of the leaders of this movement). In 1215 an independent university was founded in Paris. The *Sorbonne* (1253), although the most famous, was just one of many colleges to which students flocked from all over France. The university and its students formed an independent body which was very hostile to any perceived interference by higher authorities. This was as great a source of irritation for kings in the late Middle Ages as it was for de Gaulle during the events of May 1968.

The university system is now decentralised. There are around 200,000 students in the Paris region, distributed among thirteen universities. However, students are still firmly entrenched in the Latin Quarter.

Left: Boulevard St-Germain

Boulevard St-Michel

The so-called 'Boul Mich', laid out by Georges Eugène Haussmann, is the chief thoroughfare of the Latin Quarter, the main artery from which everything seems to flow; cafés, restaurants, bookshops and clothes shops abound, as do young people of all kinds and colours. Even those who are not genuine students are at least determined to lead as carefree a student life as possible.

A fixed sightseeing route would be inimical to the spirit of the place. Wander up and down the boulevard, keeping your eyes open, and you will always discover something to interest you – for example the small streets around *St-Séverin* which are filled with buskers in the evening (see page 13) and where there are numerous couscous restaurants; or the church of *St-Julien-le-Pauvre*, one of the oldest in Paris (1165–1220), in its quiet corner from which there is the most beautiful view across to Notre-Dame. Then there is the *Hôtel de Cluny*, once the town house of the abbots of Cluny in Burgundy, and its fine museum (see page 22); the *Collège de France* in the *Rue des Ecoles*, the most important of all learned institutions in France, and, close by, the grey bulk of the *Sorbonne*; and finally the *Panthéon*, begun in the 18th c. as a church and completed as a burial place for distinguished citizens.

Returning to the 'Boul Mich', you will inevitably come to the enchanting *Jardin du Luxembourg* (see pages 19 and 62), in which you should take a walk before continuing in the direction of St-Germain-des-Prés. On the way you will pass the *Place de l'Odéon* with the *Théâtre National de l'Odéon*, where Jean-Louis Barrault and Madeleine

Renaud made a great impact with their productions in the sixties, before they fell from grace for sympathising with the rebellious students of May 1968. You might also make a detour to *St-Sulpice*, a typical, somewhat oppressive Baroque church, with a square in front which imparts a curiously provincial atmosphere to the area.

Boulevard St-Germain

This is the other major street of the Latin Quarter, also very animated, particularly in the *Place St-Germain-des-Prés*.

The church of *St-Germain-des-Prés* has a long history. Parts of the building date from the Merovingian period. Some of the Merovingian kings were buried here, before St-Denis became the burial place of the Frankish kings. In its present form, the church dates predominantly from the 11th and 12th c., with a few 17th c. alterations and additions. The Early Gothic choir, with an ambulatory and radiating chapels, is of particular interest.

However, St-Germain-des-Prés is associated in many people's minds not with churches but with the Existentialists who, in the post-war period, congregated in the bars and cafés around the church, engaging in debate and terrifying upright citizens. Their favourite cafés were the *Flore* and the *Deux Magots*.

Once again, the contrasts are astonishing. Behind the church, the *Rue de Fürstemberg* and the small square of the same name form one of the most idyllic spots in the teeming city. The painter Eugène Delacroix had his studio here. The narrow streets between the Boulevard St-Germain and the Seine belong to the fine arts. This is the area of the *Ecole des Beaux-Arts*, and a centre for small, select art-dealers.

St-Séverin

Paris – a classified directory

The Place de la Concorde at night

 Some distinctive features

(See also pages 15–17)

Bibliothèque Nationale (French National Library): With many manuscripts, incunabula (books printed before 1500) and about 9 million volumes, the most comprehensive library in the world. Temporary exhibitions. The Reading Room (access only with reader's ticket) is an elegant iron construction dating from 1868. 58 Rue de Richelieu; Métro: Richelieu-Drouot. (Weekdays: 9 am–6 pm.)

The Catacombs: This labyrinthine series of underground limestone quarries provided building materials for Paris from Gallo-Roman times onwards. In the 1780s they were converted into a charnel-house for bones removed from Paris graveyards. Entrance: 1 Place Denfert-Rochereau; Métro: Denfert-Rochereau. (Tues.–Fri. 2–4 pm, Sat., Sun. 9–11 am, 2–4 pm, closed Mondays and public holidays.) Bring a torch!

Montmartre Cemetery: Graves of the Goncourt brothers, Heinrich Heine, Hector Berlioz, Offenbach, Stendhal, Zola, Degas, Nijinsky and Sacha Guitry. Main entrance: Av Rachel; Métro: Clichy.

Père-Lachaise Cemetery: Main entrance Bd de Ménilmontant; Métro: Père-Lachaise. (Mar. 16th to Nov. 15th 7.30 am–6 pm; Nov. 16th to Mar. 15th 8 am–5.30 pm.)

Les Egouts (the Paris sewers): Part of the sewer system may be visited by boat. A macabre, foul-smelling experience. Entrance at the corner of the Pont d'Alma and the Quai d'Orsay; Métro: Alma-Marceau. (Mon. and Wed. and the last Sat. in the month, 2–5 pm. Closed when raining.)

The striking architecture of the Forum des Halles

Forum des Halles: The 'hole' left behind by the Halles after their transfer to Rungis has become a modern shopping district, whose trendy architecture is still the object of considerable criticism. Métro: Rambuteau, Châtelet-Les Halles.

Gare de Lyon: Sumptuously decorated railway station dating from 1899, with a tower 65 m high and a gigantic clock. Bd Diderot; Métro: Gare de Lyon.

Manufacture des Gobelins: Tapestries and carpets are woven to old patterns at this factory, which has been a state institution for over 300 years. Open to the public. 42 Av des Gobelins; Métro: Gobelins. (Guided tours Tues.–Fri., 2 pm and 2.45 pm.)

Jardin des Plantes: These botanical gardens were founded in 1626 under Louis XIII as a 'physic garden' for medicinal herbs. Very attractive grounds with more than 10,000 varieties of plants, a winter garden, an alpine garden and a maze. Main entrance: Place Valhubert; Métro: Gare d'Orléans-Austerlitz. (Daily 9 am–7 pm, in winter 9 am–5 pm.)

Canal St-Martin: The canal in the east of Paris was completed in 1825. Métro: Jean-Jaurès, Place de la République, Place de la Bastille.

Marché aux Puces: The flea-market at the *Porte de Clignancourt* (Sat., Sun. and Mon.) has become the model for all flea-markets the world over. More than 2,000 stalls, and many Paris antique-dealers have branches here. Picturesque, but few bargains. Métro: Porte de Clignancourt. Less famous and smaller, but more charming, are the flea-markets at the *Porte de Montreuil* (Sat. and Sun.), Métro: Montreuil; at *Porte Didot* (Sun.), Métro: Porte de Vanves; and at the *Place d'Aligre* (daily except Mon.), Métro: Ledru Rollin.

Parc de la Villette: On the extensive area until recently covered by the Paris abattoirs and cattle-market a huge theme park is being built. The main attractions: Adrien Fainsilber's *Cité des Sciences et de l'Industrie*, a museum of science and technology reminiscent of a space station, three times as large as the Pompidou Centre and created to be the largest and most modern of its kind in the world, with an endless range of opportunities for making technology more understandable; the large, spherical cinema *La Géode* for 3-D documentary films; the *Grande Halle*, the former cattle-market, now completely restored and intended for use as an exhibition space; and finally the *Zénith* concert hall for pop and rock music, with seats for 6,000 people. By the early 1990s the large complexes of the *Cité de la Musique* (the music college) and the theatre will be operational. Between the various cultural buildings are playgrounds, footpaths, amusement parks and all kinds of functional buildings such as cafés, cinemas and shops, all intended to increase profitability. The whole complex, designed by the Swiss architect Bernard Tschumi, constantly reminds the visitor that the third millennium is just around the corner. It seems to be an unwritten law of the Parc de la Villette that, since Paris has countless temples dedicated to the cult of nostalgia, there should be no trace of it here! 26 Av Corentin Cariou. Métro: Porte de Pantin, Porte de la Villette. (Tel. 42 40 27 28 for information on the various opening times.)

Pont Alexandre III: A lavishly decorated bridge over the Seine built, like the nearby Grand Palais, for the 1900 International Exhibition. Métro: Invalides.

Pont Neuf: A bridge over the Seine that crosses the western tip of the Île de la Cité. The oldest remaining bridge in Paris, built in 1604. Métro: Pont Neuf. (See page 55.)

Tour Maine-Montparnasse: Métro: Montparnasse-Bienvenue. (Summer 9.30 am–11.30 pm, winter 10 am–10 pm.)

Parc de la Villette

Castles, palaces and parks

(See also pages 18, 19)

Bois de Boulogne: Large recreation area in the west of Paris. Roads, footpaths and bridle paths, 2 racecourses (Longchamp, Auteuil), 7 lakes (rowing boats for hire), as well as flower gardens, swimming pools, a tennis stadium, children's playgrounds, cafés, restaurants and a zoo in the Jardin d'Acclimatation. Métro: Porte Dauphine, Porte Maillot, Porte d'Auteuil.

Bois de Vincennes: A park in the south-east of Paris, at 935 ha larger than the Bois de Boulogne, but less fashionable and thus less visited. Roads, footpaths and bridle paths, sports grounds, velodrome, two artificial lakes with islands, zoo with cliffs 70 m high, playgrounds, amusement parks, cafés, restaurants. Métro: Château de Vincennes, Porte de Charenton, Porte Dorée. (See also below under Château de Vincennes.)

Champ de Mars: Laid out in 1765 as a parade ground. It is 1 km long and 500 m wide, and has been converted into a park. During the Revolutionary period, numerous festivals and demonstrations were held here. Métro: Ecole Militaire. (See page 32.)

Grand Palais: Built in 1899 by Girault in the French classical style. Lavishly decorated with sculptures. Imposing statues of horse-drawn chariots on the corner projections. Exhibitions. Métro: Champs-Elysées-Clemenceau. (Daily 10 am–8 pm, Wed. 10 am–10 pm.)

Jardin du Luxembourg: Extends over an area of 22 ha on the edge of the Latin Quarter. Garden in the formal French style, with octagonal pond and fountain, encircled by two terraces with balustrades. Greenhouses with 25,000 plants. Memorials to Flaubert, Baudelaire, Stendhal, Verlaine, George Sand. Typical 'Left Bank' atmosphere. Métro: Port Royal and Luxembourg.

Château de Vincennes: The first castle here was built in the 12th c., and was used at various times as a royal residence, a fortress and a hunting lodge. The present building is surrounded by a defensive wall and four small towers. Entrance through the *Tour de Village*. On the west side is the 14th c. *donjon* (keep), 52 m high and a fine example of the French military architecture of the period. Opposite is the *Chapelle Royale*, built in the Late

Sculpture on the Grand Palais

Longchamp – racecourse in the Bois de Boulogne

Gothic style (1364–80), with fine Renaissance windows. To the south are the two pavilions built by Mazarin around 1650 (*Pavillon du Roi, Pavillon de la Reine*). Exit through the *Tour du Bois* and over the bridge. On the other side of the main road is the Bois de Vincennes. Métro: Château de Vincennes. (The keep and Royal Chapel are open daily except on certain public holidays. Winter 10 am–5 pm, summer 9.30 am–7 pm.)

Jardin des Tuileries: A formal garden in the French classical style, 925 m long and 325 m wide, laid out under Louis XIV around 1664 by the famous landscape gardener Le Nôtre. Central avenue with spectacular views of the Louvre and the Arc de Triomphe. The gardens are laid out in strict geometric shapes, with three circular ponds and one ornately decorated octagonal pond. On the west side are two raised terraces with fine views of the Place de la Concorde and the Champs-Elysées. Next to the terraces are the Orangerie and the Jeu de Paume. Métro: Tuileries, Place de la Concorde.

Palais Bourbon: Palace of the Duchess of Bourbon, a daughter of Louis XIV and Madame de Montespan; built in 1722. Beautiful inner courtyard from the period of Louis XVI. In 1807 the façade was rebuilt on Napoleon's orders in the classical style, so that it would match that of the Madeleine. In the library, allegorical ceiling-paintings by Delacroix (1838–45). The palace is now the seat of the French National Assembly. Métro: Chambre des Députés. (The interior may be visited only with written permission from the secretariat of the National Assembly.)

Palais de Chaillot: Built on the occasion of the 1937 World Exhibition. It contains several museums and the Théâtre National de Chaillot. A wonderful view from the terrace over the Eiffel Tower, Champ de Mars and Ecole Militaire. Métro: Trocadéro.

Palais de l'Elysée: Built in 1718 for the Count of Evreux; frequent changes of ownership. Former occupants include Madame de Pompadour and the Empress Josephine. Since 1873 it has been the official residence of the president of the French Republic. Métro: Champs-Elysées. No admission.

Palais du Louvre: The original building was one of Philippe Auguste's fortresses (c. 1200), which Charles V made into a royal residence in the mid-14th c. During the Renaissance, François I had a new palace built on the site; parts of the buildings around the Cour Carrée in fact date from the 16th c. The 17th c. saw the construction of the Pavillon de l'Horloge (Lemercier, 1624) and the

The Palais de Chaillot

massive colonnades on the east façade (1667–73, Perrault). Building came to a halt when Louis XIV moved his court to Versailles, and was only resumed under Napoleon I and completed under Napoleon III. Most of the huge palace is now occupied by the Musée du Louvre (see pages 51, 70). Métro: Louvre.

Palais du Luxembourg: In 1612 Maria de' Medici acquired the palace of the Duke of Luxembourg (hence the name) and had the present palace built (1615–25) by de Brosse on the site. She only occupied it for a short time, however, because she was banished from France by her son, Louis XIII, in 1630. Prior to this she had commissioned twenty-one large paintings by Rubens depicting scenes from her life; they now hang in the Louvre. The palace is now the seat of the Senate, the upper chamber of the French parliament. Métro: Odéon and Luxembourg. No admission at the moment. (For information tel. 42 34 20 60.)

Parc Bagatelle: In 1775 the Count of Artois entered into a wager with his sister-in-law, Marie-Antoinette, that he could 'conjure up' a little château in an English park within three months. The park owes its existence to this wager. Marvellous displays of flowers in the spring and summer. Part of the Bois de Boulogne (see page 62). (Winter 9 am–5 pm, summer 8.30 am–7 pm.)

Parc des Buttes-Chaumont: Commissioned by Napoleon III and laid out by Haussmann between 1864 and 1867, this lies well away from all the main tourist attractions. The picturesque park covers 23 ha, and has a lake and island, two bridges and a circular temple in the classical style. Métro: Buttes-Chaumont.

Parc Monceau: This small, charming, very Parisian park lies in the north-west of the city. It is laid out in romantic style, with fine old trees, mock ruins, a small lake and statues of famous French people. Métro: Monceau.

Parc Montsouris: Opposite the Cité Universitaire, a sort of counterpart to the Parc des Buttes-Chaumont. Métro: Cité Universitaire.

Parc de la Villette: see page 61.

Architecture

(See also pages 20, 21, 32)

Arc de Triomphe: A large triumphal arch, built at the wish of Napoleon to honour the French army (1806–36). 50 m high, 45 m wide, viewing platform. The façades are adorned with groups of figures and reliefs depicting historical military scenes. Under the arch is the Tomb of the Unknown Soldier, whose flame is relit each evening. In the upper storey is a small museum displaying items associated with the construction of the monument. (See also page 51.) Métro: Charles-de-Gaulle. (Museum and platform open in summer 10 am–5.30 pm, in winter 10 am–5 pm. Closed on certain public holidays.)

Arc de Triomphe du Carrousel: Erected between 1806 and 1808 in honour of Napoleon's victories; on the platform is a bronze chariot group by Bosio. Splendid view along the 'Triumphal Way' to the Arc de Triomphe. Métro: Palais Royal.

L'Arche de la Défense, also known as **La Grande Arche:** Designed by the Danish architect von Spreckelsen. The space under the 110-m-high cube, which stands at the end of the axis running from the Louvre through the Tuileries, the Champs-Elysées and the Arc de Triomphe, would accommodate the cathedral of Notre-Dame. Since its inauguration on July 14th 1989, the 'Arc de Triomphe de l'Humanité' has been used mainly by organisations seeking a prestigious address, and, on a more exalted level, for a Foundation of Human Rights. The 'cloud' of fabric awnings that hangs inside the hollow space is intended to protect visitors from the permanent draught and to act as a light filter. The arch stands at an angle of 6 degrees to the historic axis, as does its counterpart at the other end, the pyramid in the Cour Napoléon in the Louvre. As a result, when viewed from the city the cube is seen in three dimensions. The new suburb of La Défense owes its name to a modest monument commemorating the defence of Paris in 1871. Métro-RER: La Défense.

L'Arche de la Défense

Conciergerie: A fortress-like palace on the Île de la Cité. Impressive north façade (best view from the Quai de la Mégisserie) with four squat towers; the crenellated Tour de Bonbec is the oldest, while the Tour de l'Horloge (Clock Tower) is the most famous. It was here that the first public clock in Paris was installed, in 1370. Interior: *Salle des Gens d'Armes*, an impressive four-aisled hall, once the servants' dining hall and recreation room; *Salle des Gardes*, the guardroom with massive vaulting-pillars and beautiful capitals; various rooms where prisoners were held, and a gigantic kitchen which at times catered for a royal household of more than 2,000 people. Entrance: 1 Quai de l'Horloge. Métro: Cité. (Daily 10 am–4.30 pm in winter, 9.30 am–5.30 pm in summer. Closed on certain public holidays.)

Dôme des Invalides: A building typical of the classical period of French architecture (17th c.). Built for Louis XIV (1679–1706) and designed by Hardouin-Mansart as a symbol of the glory of the French monarchy. A Baroque structure in the manner of St Peter's in Rome. Two-storeyed façade, decorated with Greek columns, and a particularly splendid dome roofed with lead and adorned with gilded trophies. The ground-plan takes the form of a Greek cross. Beneath the dome in the open crypt is Napoleon's tomb, a sarcophagus of red porphyry. The Emperor's remains are contained in a coffin of six layers made, respectively, of tinplate, mahogany, lead, lead again, ebony and oak. Over the entrance to the crypt is inscribed the Emperor's dying wish: 'I desire that my ashes rest on the banks of the Seine, in the midst of the French people whom I have loved so dearly.' In the background is the tomb of Napoleon's son, duke of Reichstadt and king of Rome. Métro: Ecole Militaire. (Daily in winter 10 am–5 pm, in summer 10 am–6 pm. Closed on certain public holidays.)

Ecole Militaire: A military school founded by Louis XV for the training of future general staff officers. Métro: Trocadéro and Ecole Militaire.

Eiffel Tower: This masterpiece of steel construction has been preserved as a reminder of the 1889 International Exhibition. Height 300 m (see page 15). Métro: Bir-Hakeim, Trocadéro, Champ de Mars. (Daily 10 am–11 pm.)

Faubourg St-Germain: A former suburb with many 18th c. mansions. Métro: Chambre des Députés.

Hôtel de Cluny: Built in 1485 as the Paris residence of the abbots of Cluny. One of the few surviving secular Gothic buildings in the city. Musée de Cluny (see page 22). Métro: St-Michel. (Museum open daily 9.45 am–12.30 pm and 2–5.15 pm, except Tues. and public holidays.)

Hôtel des Invalides: Founded by Louis XIV as a home for disabled soldiers. It houses the *Musée de l'Armée*, the church of St-Louis-des-Invalides, the Musée des Plans-Reliefs, containing some 80 models of fortresses of historical interest, and the Museum of the Order of Liberation. Métro: Invalides. (Opening hours as for the Dôme des Invalides.)

Hôtel de Sens: A part-Gothic, part-Renaissance mansion built for the archbishop of Sens and the bishop of Paris (1475–1507). Apart from the Hôtel de Cluny, the only remaining private residence from the late Middle Ages. It houses the *Bibliothèque Forney*, which has a valuable collection of copperplate engravings and books about French

Notre-Dame-de-Paris

crafts. 1 Rue de Figuier. Métro: Pont Marie. (Library: Tues.–Fri. 1.30–8.30 pm, Sat. 10 am–8.30 pm. Closed Sun., Mon. and public holidays.)

Hôtel de Ville (Town Hall): Built in the neo-Renaissance style (1874–82) to replace the old town hall destroyed during the Paris Commune of 1871. Métro: Hôtel de Ville. (Guided tour Mon. 10.30 am.)

La Madeleine (Eglise Ste-Marie-Madeleine): The church, begun in 1764, stands imposingly at one end of the Rue Royale. Métro: Madeleine.

Le Marais: Former residential district of the nobility with many 17th and 18th c. town mansions (*hôtels*). (See page 46.)

Notre-Dame-de-Paris: The cathedral of Paris, and one of the most important of Gothic buildings. The former sacristy now contains the Treasury. (See page 54.) Métro: Cité. (Daily: *Treasury* 10 am–6 pm, Sun. and public holidays 2–6 pm; *Crypt* 10 am–5.30 pm in summer, 10 am–4.30 pm in winter, 9.30 am–6.30 pm July/August. Closed on certain public holidays.)

Opéra (the old Opera House): Built between 1862 and 1875 by Charles Garnier as the largest opera house in the world. The building also houses the Museum of Opera and a library which contains the scores of all operas and ballets performed here. (See pages 33, 43.) Métro: Opéra. (Daily 11 am–4.30 pm. Closed on public holidays.)

Opéra Bastille (New Opera House): Inaugurated on July 14th 1989, the bicentenary of the French Revolution. The colossal concrete and glass building, with a seating capacity of 2,800 (almost four times that of the old Opéra), looms massively over the Place de la Bastille. Métro: Bastille.

Panthéon: Originally designed as a church (1758, Soufflot), but in 1791 the

The Panthéon

Constituent Assembly decided that it should become a pantheon, a final resting place for the 'mortal remains of the great men of France's liberty'. In the crypt are the tombs of Rousseau, Voltaire, Soufflot, Hugo, Jaurès and Zola. Of particular interest is the majestic dome. Métro: Cardinal-Lemoine and Luxembourg. (Daily 10 am–5.30 pm in summer, 10 am–noon and 2–5 pm in winter. Closed on certain public holidays.)

Sacré-Coeur: Basilica in a Romanesque-Byzantine style on top of the Butte Montmartre, built between 1876 and 1910 as an expiatory offering and dedicated to the Sacred Heart of Jesus. The white dome and the bell-tower are now part of the Paris skyline. Ornate mosaic decoration in its dark interior. Splendid view from the outer gallery over Paris and the surrounding area. Métro: Anvers. (Dome and gallery open daily 9.15 am–6.30 pm, from Oct. to Palm Sunday 9 am–5 pm.)

St-Denis: This basilica to the north of Paris was begun in 1137 and consecrated in 1281. It was here that the Gothic style first emerged. Métro: Line 18 (suburban tariff) St-Denis-Basilique.

St-Etienne-du-Mont: In 1220 the abbey church of Ste-Geneviève stood on the hill. As it became too small, the parish church of St-Etienne was built next to it. Constantly extended from 1492 and finally consecrated in 1626, this remarkable edifice has a High Gothic choir and nave and a Renaissance façade. The fine rood screen (1521–35) between the nave and the choir, with its Renaissance decoration, is one of the few of its kind remaining in France. Métro: Cardinal-Lemoine.

St-Eustache: Church on the edge of the district of les Halles, built between 1532 and 1637, and reckoned one of the most beautiful in Paris. Métro: Les Halles.

St-Germain-des-Prés: The oldest church in Paris. The bell-tower and parts of the nave and transept date from the 11th c. (see page 58). Métro: St-Germain-des-Prés.

St-Germain-l'Auxerrois: Building work on this church, which stands opposite the east façade of the Louvre, went on from the 12th to the 17th c. A veritable museum of architectural history. Métro: Louvre.

St-Julien-le-Pauvre: Church in the Latin Quarter, built between 1165 and 1220, at about the same time as Notre-Dame. However, it is predominantly Romanesque in style. The façade was rebuilt in the 17th c. Métro: St-Michel.

St-Louis-en-l'Île: Church on the Île St-Louis (1664–1726). Baroque interior in white and gold. Alabaster reliefs from the 14th and 15th c. Métro: Pont Marie.

Right: Sculptures, Notre-Dame
Left: The Sacré-Coeur

St-Séverin: Church in the Latin Quarter, begun in the 13th c. (main doorway and the first three bays in the nave), nave and choir 14th to 16th c. The strikingly wide church has no transept. Richly decorated double ambulatory in the Late Gothic style, sumptuously coloured windows in the nave (15th c.). Numerous votive pictures, with which students in the Latin Quarter give thanks for 'divine assistance' in their examinations. Métro: St-Michel. (Mon.–Fri. 11 am–1 pm and 3.30–7.30 pm.)

St-Sulpice: Church in the square of the same name, extended and renovated between 1646 and 1732. The façade is in the monumental classical style, as are the towers. First side-chapel on the right: three frescos (1849–61) by Delacroix. Lady Chapel: statue of the Virgin Mary standing on a globe, by Pigalle. Fine organ front (1776). Remarkable holy-water stoups

near the entrance: the huge shells were presented to François I by the city of Venice. Métro: St-Sulpice.

Sainte-Chapelle: Gothic chapel in the Palais de Justice, built between 1245 and 1248 as a palace chapel for Louis IX (see page 54). Métro: Cité. (In summer 9.30 am–6.15 pm, in winter 10.15 am–4.45 pm. Closed on certain public holidays.)

Tour St-Jacques: The Late Gothic tower is all that remains of the church of St-Jacques-la-Boucherie (1508–22). The statue of Pascal is a memorial to his experiment, conducted on the tower, to determine the weight of air (1648). Métro: Hôtel de Ville, Châtelet.

Val-de-Grâce: Extensive monastery buildings south of the Latin Quarter with an impressive domed church in the tradition of Roman ecclesiastical architecture (1645–67, Hardouin-Mansart, Lemercier and Le Duc). Métro: Port Royal.

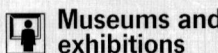

Museums and exhibitions

(See also page 51)

Musée du Louvre

The museum, probably the richest and most beautiful collection of art treasures in the world, owes its origins to François I (early 16th c.) and was constantly expanded in the centuries that followed, notably by Louis XIV, Louis XVI and Napoleon I. It is estimated that the museum now has approximately 400,000 exhibits. The complete renovation and restructuring of the museum (of which the glass entrance pyramid is a distinctive symbol; see page 52) will carry on into the mid-1990s. Despite the consequent alterations and closures, you will still find more than enough to interest you.

Apart from the main entrance in the pyramid in the Cour Napoléon, there are other entrances in the Place du Palais Royal/Rue de Rivoli and at Porte Jaujard. Métro: Palais Royal. (Daily except Tues. 9 am–6 pm; Mon. and Wed. until 9.45 pm. Some departments closed between 12.30 and 2 pm. Admission free on Sun.)

The following description can only hint at the riches housed in the Louvre. Take note of the up-to-date information in the entrance hall and in the English guidebooks.

The collections in the Louvre are divided into six departments: Greek and Roman antiquities, Oriental antiquities, Egyptian antiquities, European paintings and drawings, European sculpture and objets d'art.

Greek and Roman antiquities: The finest items are concentrated in the *Salle archaïque* (Archaic Greek art from the 7th–5th c. BC), *Salle du Parthénon* (Greek Early Classical of the 5th c. BC, including fragments of the Parthenon at Athens), *Salle de Phidias* and *Salle de Polyclète* (Classical period with works by Phidias and Polykleitos, c. 450–390 BC), *Salle de Praxitèle* and *Salle de Lysippe* (Late Classical period with works by Praxiteles and Lysippus, c. 390–330 BC) and the *Salle de la Vénus de Milo*, with the celebrated sculpture of a female torso (2nd c. BC) found on the island of Melos. Also from the Hellenistic period is the Nike of Samothrace which stands on the *Escalier Daru*, the big staircase leading to the first floor.

Oriental antiquities: The richest collection of Middle Eastern objects from Babylon (between the Euphrates and the Tigris), Susa (east of the Tigris), Persia, Mari and Phoenicia. The most outstanding objects include the famous

Codex of Hammurabi, the oldest known legal text (c. 2000 BC) – a huge block of black basalt in which is inscribed the text of 282 laws; also the 'Frieze of the Archers of the King of Persia', made of enamelled brick (6th c. BC).

Egyptian antiquities: The most important works of Egyptian sculpture are on display on the ground floor. In the crypt under the Pavillon des Arts is a large sphinx of pink granite (Middle Kingdom). In Room 5 is the statue of a scribe sitting cross-legged (c. 3000 BC), one of the most famous surviving works from the Old Kingdom.

European paintings and drawings: This is the most popular department in the Louvre and certainly the most comprehensive collection of European painting in the world.

The *French School* is represented by painters from Fouquet and Clouet to Ingres and Delacroix, including Watteau, Boucher and Fragonard.

The *Italian School* is represented by Giotto, Fra Angelico, Uccello, Mantegna, Leonardo da Vinci (*Mona Lisa*), Raphael, Titian, Tintoretto, Caravaggio and others.

From the *Flemish School* there are Van Eyck, Memling, Bosch, Rubens and Van Dyck. The major painter of the *Dutch School* represented here is Rembrandt; there are also works by Hals and Van Goyen.

The *German School* is represented by Dürer, Cranach the Elder and Holbein, and the *Spanish School* by El Greco, Velázquez and Murillo.

European sculpture: The emphasis of this collection is on French Romanesque, Gothic and Renaissance sculpture. Of particular note among the sculptures from the rest of Europe are Michelangelo's famous *Slaves*, intended for the tomb of Pope Julius II (*Salle Michelangelo*).

Objets d'art: This department contains collections of furniture, tapestries, glass and porcelain from French châteaux, as well as ivory-, silver- and enamelwork by outstanding craftsmen.

Other museums

Centre Georges-Pompidou or Centre Beaubourg:
Art by famous 20th c. masters. Rue Rambuteau, corner of Rue St-Martin. Métro: Rambuteau. (Daily except Tues. noon–10 pm, Sat., Sun. and public holidays 10 am–10 pm.) (See also Musée National d'Art Moderne, below.)

Musée de l'Armée:
Weapons and uniforms of the French Army from the Middle Ages to the Second World War, flags, maps of campaigns, and medieval armour and weapons. Hôtel des Invalides, Place des Invalides. Métro: Invalides. (Daily in summer 10 am–6 pm, in winter 10 am–5 pm. Closed on certain public holidays.)

Musée d'Art Moderne de la Ville de Paris:
The collection in the Museum of Modern Art of the City of Paris contains mainly paintings, including works by Braque, Derain, Dufy, Matisse, Modigliani, Rouault, Utrillo. 11 Av du Président-Wilson. Métro: Alma-Marceau. (Daily except Mon. 10 am–5.30 pm, Wed. till 8.30 pm.)

Musée National d'Art Moderne:
The National Museum of Modern Art, now housed in the Pompidou Centre, contains a huge collection of 20th c. art, with the main emphasis on pointillism, fauvism, surrealism, dadaism, expressionism and abstract and contemporary artists. Various temporary exhibitions. Métro: Rambuteau. (Daily except Tues. noon–10 pm, Sat. and Sun. 10 am–10 pm. Tel. 42 77 12 33.)

Musée des Arts Décoratifs: A museum of decorative and ornamental art, 107 Rue de Rivoli. Métro: Palais Royal. (Daily Wed.–Sat. 12.30–6 pm, Sun. 11 am–6 pm.)

Musée Balzac: Mementos of the writer Honoré de Balzac. 47 Rue Raynouard. Métro: Passy. (Daily except Mon. and public holidays 10 am–5.40 pm.)

Musée (Hôtel) Carnavalet: A museum illustrating the history of Paris. 23 Rue de Sévigné. Métro: St-Paul. (Daily except Mon. and certain public holidays 10 am–5.40 pm, free admission on Sun.)

Musée National de Céramique: China and porcelain from all over the world. In Sèvres; Métro: Pont de Sèvres. (Daily except Tues. 9.45 am–noon and 1.30–5.15 pm.)

Musée (Hôtel) de Cluny: Medieval and Renaissance arts and crafts. 6 Place Paul Painlevé. Métro: St-Michel.

The Pompidou Centre

(Daily except Tues. and public holidays 9.45 am–noon and 2–5.15 pm.)

Musée Cognacq-Jay: 18th c. European works of art, including paintings by Boucher, Fragonard, Canaletto and Gainsborough. Former address: 25 Bd des Capucines; should now have reopened in the Hôtel Donon, 8 Rue Elzévir. Métro: St-Paul.

Musée Delacroix: Works by and mementos of the painter. 6 Rue de Fürstemberg. Métro: St-Germain-des-Prés. (Daily except Tues. and public holidays 10 am–5.15 pm, Dec.–Mar. closed between 12.30 and 1.30 pm.)

Musée d'Ennery: Oriental art (furniture, porcelain, lacquer-work and jade). 59 Av Foch. Métro: Victor-Hugo, Porte Dauphine. (Thurs. and Sun. 2–5 pm; closed in August.)

Musée Guimet: Works of art from India, Cambodia, Nepal, Tibet, China, Japan and Korea. 6 Place d'Iéna. Métro: Iéna. (Daily except Tues. and public holidays 9.45 am–noon and 1.30–5.15 pm.)

Musée Victor Hugo: The writer's former residence, with many mementos. 6 Place des Vosges (see page 47). Métro: Bastille, Chemin-Vert. (Daily except Mon. and public holidays 10 am–5.40 pm.)

Musée Jacquemart-André: Art and artefacts, particularly from the French Rococo period and the Italian Renaissance. Métro: Miromesnil. (Daily except Mon., Tues. and public holidays 1.30–5.30 pm; closed in August.)

Musée de la Marine: A comprehensive survey of French naval history. Palais de Chaillot. Métro: Trocadéro. (Daily except Tues. 10 am–6 pm.)

Musée Marmottan: Works of art of the Renaissance and Empire periods, as well as paintings by Monet and other Impressionists. 2 Rue Louis-Boilly. Métro: Muette. (Daily except Mon. 10 am–5.30 pm.)

Cabinet des Médailles et des Antiques: Medals, coins and gems. 58 Rue de Richelieu (Bibliothèque Nationale). Métro: Richelieu-Drouot. (Daily except Sun. and public holidays 1–5 pm.)

Musée de Montmartre: Mementos of the great period of bohemian life in Montmartre. 12 Rue Cortot. Métro: Lamarck-Caulaincourt. (Daily except Mon. 2.30–5.30 pm, Sun. 11 am–6 pm.)

Musée d'Orsay: Painting, sculpture, photography, film, design, furniture and other exhibits from the period between 1848 and 1914, as well as architectural models. 1 Rue de Bellechasse. Métro: Solférino. (Daily except Mon. 10 am–6 pm, Thurs. 10 am–9.45 pm, Sun. 9 am–6 pm.)

Musée du Petit Palais (also Musée des Beaux-Arts de la Ville de Paris): Works of art from the Middle Ages and the Renaissance, and 19th and early 20th c. French paintings. Petit Palais, Av Winston-Churchill. Métro: Champs-Elysées-Clemenceau. (Daily except Mon. and public holidays 10 am–5.40 pm.)

Musée Picasso: The largest Picasso collection in the world! Hôtel Salé, 5 Rue de Thorigny. Métro: St-Paul, Chemin-Vert. (Daily except Tues. 9.15 am–5.15 pm, Wed. until 10 pm.)

Musée Rodin: Major works by this sculptor, and temporary exhibitions. The garden of the museum is also worth a visit. 77 Rue de Varenne. Métro: Varenne, Rue du Bac. (Daily except Tues. 10 am–5.45 pm in summer, 10 am–5 pm in winter. Closed May 1st and Dec. 25th.)

Food and drink

(See also pages 25–29)

De luxe restaurants (from about 400 F per head)

Taillevent: In absolutely the highest class for many years. Enchanting *Belle Epoque* décor. A restaurant in the very best Parisian tradition. 15 Rue Lamennais, tel. 45 61 12 90. Métro: George V.
Lucas Carton: Chef Alain Senderens is one of the great masters of French haute cuisine. A temple of gastronomy with original décor dating from 1900. 9 Place Madeleine, tel. 42 65 22 90. Métro: Madeleine.
Tour d'Argent: Famous for its duck, a magnificent view over Notre-Dame and a splendid wine cellar. A first-class 'traditional' restaurant. 15 Quai Tournelle, tel. 43 54 23 31. Métro: Maubert-Mutualité.
Grand Véfour: One of the most beautiful restaurants in France and probably the oldest in Paris, with its original *Directoire* décor, and very tradition-conscious cuisine. 17 Rue Beaujolais, tel. 42 96 56 27. Métro: Bourse.
Jamin: Many knowledgeable people consider the *patron*, Joel Robuchon, a genius and his restaurant the best in Paris at the moment. The ambience is modern and very elegant. 32 Rue de Longchamp, tel. 47 27 12 27. Métro: Trocadéro.

Restaurants and bistros with good French cooking from about 150 F per head

Allard: Bistro. Madame does the cooking, Monsieur serves! 41 Rue St-André-des-Arts, tel. 43 26 48 23. Métro: St-Michel.
Benoît: Original 1900s décor, straight

out of a picture book! 20 Rue St-Martin, tel. 42 72 25 76. Métro: Rambuteau.

Le Bistrot de Paris: A genuine, typical bistro from around the turn of the century. Famous for its *foie gras*. 33 Rue de Lille, tel. 42 61 16 83. Métro: Quai d'Orsay.

Bofinger: Said to be the oldest brasserie in Paris. Very fashionable again following the gentrification of the Bastille district. Seafood always fresh. 5 Rue de la Bastille, tel. 42 72 87 82. Métro: Bastille.

Flo: Agreeable, honest food in a brasserie with original *Belle Epoque* décor. 63 Rue du Faubourg-St-Denis, tel. 47 70 13 59. Métro: Strasbourg/St-Denis.

Dodin Bouffant: Informal atmosphere, excellent fish dishes, good value for money. 25 Rue Frédéric-Sauton, tel. 43 25 25 14. Métro: Maubert-Mutualité.

Julien: Fashionable, elegant restaurant in slightly dubious neighbourhood. Fine *Belle Epoque* décor. Specialities: *foie gras* and salmon pâté. 16 Rue du Faubourg-St-Denis, tel. 47 70 12 06. Métro: Strasbourg/St-Denis.

Lipp: Hearty Alsace cooking, artistic tradition, nostalgic and authentic décor. 151 Bd St-Germain, tel. 45 48 53 91. Métro: St-Germain-des-Prés.

Mercure Galant: Has consistently offered good-quality food for many years. Exquisite salads and desserts. 15 Rue des Petits-Champs, tel. 42 97 53 85. Métro: Pyramides.

Maître Paul: Friendly, modest family-run establishment. Sample the *coq au vin*! 12 Rue Monsieur-le-Prince, tel. 43 54 74 59. Métro: Odéon.

Olympe: The Gault-Millau guide speaks of the best 'cuisine de femme' in the world! Evenings only. 8 Rue N.-Charlet, tel. 47 34 86 08. Métro: Pasteur.

Pharamond: Famous bistro, renowned for its *tripes à la mode de Caen*. Hearty Norman cuisine. 24 Rue Grande-Truanderie, tel. 42 33 06 72. Métro: Les Halles.

Chez Pauline: Good, traditional bistro cooking, although *foie gras* is also on the menu. 5 Rue Villedo, tel. 42 96 20 70. Métro: Pyramides.

Au Pied de Cochon: Popular, traditional restaurant in what was formerly les Halles. Open day and night. 6 Rue Coquillière, tel. 42 36 11 75. Métro: Les Halles.

Pierre Traiteur: Pleasant, cultivated atmosphere, fine cooking inspired by all regions of the country. 10 Rue Richelieu, tel. 42 96 09 17. Métro: Palais Royal.

Au Quai des Ormes: Slightly cool atmosphere, but excellent restaurant with an attractive first-floor terrace. Exquisite game dishes! 72 Quai-de-l'Hôtel-de-Ville, tel. 42 74 72 22. Métro: Hôtel-de-Ville.

Récamier: Elegant establishment with classic Burgundian cuisine. 4 Rue Récamier, tel. 45 48 86 58. Métro: St-Sulpice.

Polidor: Typical Rive Gauche bistro of the best sort, agreeable atmosphere, good value for money. Speciality: *escargots*. 41 Rue Monsieur-le-Prince, tel. 43 26 95 34. Métro: Odéon.

Le Petit Montmorency: Friendly bistro of the superior kind. Not exactly cheap. *Foie gras* and truffle salad highly recommended! 5 Rue Rabelais, tel. 42 25 11 19. Métro: St-Philippe-de-Roule.

A Sousceyrac: Solid, well-managed family restaurant in the Bastille district, where substance still counts for more than appearances. 35 Rue Faidherbe, tel. 43 71 65 30. Métro: Faidherbe-Chaligny.

Terminus Nord: A large, lively brasserie opposite the Gare du Nord; passable Alsace cooking. 23 Rue de Dunkerque, tel. 42 85 05 15. Métro: Gare du Nord.

Au Trou Gascon: Hearty Gascon cooking well away from the main tourist routes. 40 Rue Taine, tel. 43 44 34 26. Métro: Daumesnil.

Quick, cheap and reliable (usually under 100 F per head)

L'Assiette au Boeuf: Everything revolves around steak and salad. 22 Rue Guillaume-Apollinaire. Métro: St-Germain-des-Prés.

Chartier: Mass catering, loud, entertaining, informal and not bad. 7 Rue du Faubourg Montmartre. Métro: Montmartre.

Le Commerce-Chartier: The same deal in different surroundings! 51 Rue du Commerce. Métro: Emile Zola.

Centre Pompidou: Modern restaurant, no atmosphere, but functional. And with a view over the city! Centre Pompidou-Beaubourg. Métro: Rambuteau.

L'Ecluse: Small wine bars with choice light dishes and a good selection of wines by the glass. 15 Quai des Grands-Augustins; 15 Place de la Madeleine; 64 Rue François 1er.

Self-service restaurants (Libre-Service)

Easy to find in the city centre, particularly along the *grands boulevards* around the Opéra, near the Palais Royal, in the Latin Quarter, in Montparnasse and below the Butte Montmartre.

Opera, theatre and music

(See also pages 33, 34)

Subsidised theatres

Opéra: Place de l'Opéra; Métro: Opéra. Classical ballet.

Opéra Bastille (New Opera House): Place de la Bastille; seating capacity of 2,800. Métro: Bastille. Classical opera.

Opéra-Comique (Salle Favart): Place Boieldieu; Métro: Richelieu-Drouot. More popular programme, e.g. French and Italian opera.

Comédie-Française (Salle Richelieu): Place du Théâtre Français; Métro: Palais Royal. Classical French drama.

Odéon-Théâtre de France: Place Paul-Claudel; Métro: Odéon. Works by modern dramatists.

Théâtre National de Chaillot: Palais de Chaillot, Place du Trocadéro; Métro: Trocadéro. All types of stage plays.

Théâtre de l'Est Parisien (TEP): 17 Rue Malte-Brun; Métro: Gambetta. All types of stage plays and concerts. Culture for the benefit of the workers rather than that of the educated middle classes.

The major concert halls

Salle du Conservatoire, 2 bis Rue du Conservatoire; Métro: Bonne-Nouvelle.
Salle Gaveau, 45 Rue la Boëtie; Métro: Miromesnil.
Salle Pleyel, 252 Rue du Faubourg St-Honoré; Métro: Ternes.
Théâtre des Champs-Elysées, 15 Av Montaigne; Métro: Alma-Marceau.

Light opera

Châtelet (Théâtre Musical de Paris): Place du Châtelet; Métro: Châtelet. Operettas and musicals.

Bouffes Parisiens: 4 Rue Monsigny; Métro: 4 Septembre.

Comedy theatres

Caumartin, 25 Rue Caumartin; Métro: Madeleine.
Comédie des Champs-Elysées, 15 Av

Varenne Métro station – near the Rodin Museum

Montaigne; Métro: Alma-Marceau.
Daunou, 7 Rue Daunou; Métro: Opéra.
Gymnase, 38 Bd Bonne-Nouvelle; Métro: Bonne-Nouvelle.
Madeleine, 19 Rue du Surène; Métro: Madeleine.
Mathurins, 36 Rue des Mathurins; Métro: Havre-Caumartin.
Nouveautés, 24 Bd Poissonière; Métro: Montmartre.
Renaissance, 20 Bd St-Martin; Métro: Strasbourg/St-Denis.
Théâtre de Paris, 15 Rue Blanche; Métro: Trinité.
Théâtre de la Ville (formerly: Sarah Bernhardt), 2 Place du Châtelet; Métro: Châtelet.

Other theatres

Ambassadeurs, 1 Av Gabriel; Métro: Concorde.
Antoine, 14 Bd de Strasbourg; Métro: Strasbourg/St-Denis.
Athénée-Louis-Jouvet, Square Opéra-Louis-Jouvet; Métro: Opéra.
Capucines, 39 Bd des Capucines; Métro: Madeleine.
Cartoucheries de Vincennes, Av de la Pyramide; Métro: Château de Vincennes. The various stages, with a predominantly experimental programme, occupy the site of a former munitions factory.
Gaîté-Montparnasse, 20 Rue de la Gaîté; Métro: Gaîté.
Gramont, 30 Rue Gramont; Métro: Richelieu-Drouot.
Hébertot, 78 bis Bd des Batignolles; Métro: Rome.
Huchette, 23 Rue de la Huchette; Métro: St-Michel.
Marigny, Carré-Marigny; Métro: Clemenceau.
Palais Royal, 38 Rue de Montpensier; Métro: Palais Royal.
Poche-Montparnasse, 75 Bd Montparnasse; Métro: Montparnasse.
Variétés, 7 Bd Montmartre; Métro: Montmartre.

Paris by night

(See also pages 35–37)

The listings in the weekly *L'Officiel des Spectacles*, 2 F at all newspaper kiosks, are an indispensable guide. In addition to addresses and telephone numbers, prices, starting times and Métro stations are also indicated. Variety theatres are patronised by tourists rather than Parisians. If several starting times are listed, e.g. 9 pm and 11.30 pm, the first show is for tourists only! If a show does not even begin until after midnight, you can probably expect something pretty explosive. Unfortunately, most casinos are for members only.

Music halls, revue theatres, dîners-spectacles (also listed in the guides under 'Cabarets')

Alcazar: Intimate setting, as befits the Left Bank. Be warned: visual and verbal erotica! 62 Rue Mazarin; Métro: Odéon.

Le Crazy Horse Saloon was a meeting place for the jet set in the good old days. Now open to anyone who can afford it. 12 Av George V; Métro: George V.

Folies-Bergères and *Moulin Rouge* have concentrated on the tourist trade and restrict themselves to reworkings of tried and tested formulas. Folies-Bergères: 32 Rue Richer; Métro: Montmartre. Moulin Rouge: Place Blanche; Métro: Blanche.

Le Lido, with its lavish décor (fountains, etc.) and the pretty Bluebell Girls, is still a first-class establishment. 16 Champs-Elysées; Métro: Trinité.

Le Milliardaire: 68 Rue Pierre-Charron; Métro: George V.

Le Tabarin: 36 Rue Victor-Massé; Métro: Pigalle.

Nightclubs, discos, jazz clubs

Les Bains: Always has interesting musical performances! 7 Rue Bourg-l'Abbé; Métro: Etienne-Marcel.

Le Balajo: This newly fashionable establishment recreates the old dance-hall atmosphere of the Bastille district. 9 Rue de Lappe; Métro: Bastille.

Chapelle des Lombards: 'Music with rum', meaning Caribbean and Latin-American rhythms. A must for devotees! 19 Rue de Lappe; Métro: Bastille.

L'Eléphant Blanc: 'Respectable' Montparnasse dance hall, with terrace restaurant. 24 Rue Vavin; Métro: Vavin.

Le Fürstemberg: Typical St-Germain jazz club; there are several similar establishments in the immediate vicinity. 27 Rue de Buci; Métro: Odéon.

Golf Drouot: Live rock music and discos. 2 Rue Drouot; Métro: Richelieu-Drouot.

Keur Samba: An interesting clientèle. Predominantly black music. 79 Rue la Boëtie; Métro: St-Philippe-du-Roule.

Le Palace: For many years the leading disco in the city, located in a former cinema. A different musical programme is offered for each day of the week. 8 Rue du Faubourg-Montmartre; Métro: Montmartre.

At Regine's: For many years the favourite establishment of the fashionable set. A little in decline of late, but still rather special. 49 Rue de Ponthieu; Métro: F.-D.-Roosevelt.

Haute couture and fashion

(See also pages 38, 39)

Armani: 6 Place Vendôme; Métro: Pyramides.

Pierre Balmain: 44 Rue François Ier; Métro: George V.

Pierre Cardin: 27 Av de Marigny; Métro: Champs-Elysées-Clemenceau.

Carven: 6 Rond-Point des Champs-Elysées; Métro: F.-D.-Roosevelt.

Coco Chanel: 31 Rue Cambon; Métro: Madeleine.

Courrèges: 40 Rue François Ier; Métro: George V.

Christian Dior: 30 Av Montaigne; Métro: F.-D.-Roosevelt.

Jacques Esterel: 124 Rue du Faubourg St-Honoré; Métro: St-Philippe-du-Roule.

Louis Feraud: 88 Rue du Faubourg St-Honoré; Métro: St-Philippe-du-Roule.

Hubert de Givenchy: 3 Av George V; Métro: Alma-Marceau.

Kenzo: 3 Place des Victoires; Métro: Bourse.

Karl Lagerfeld: 19 Rue du Faubourg St-Honoré; Métro: Madeleine.

Jeanne Lanvin: 22 Rue du Faubourg St-Honoré; Métro: Concorde.

Ted Lapidus: 37 Av Pierre Ier-de-Serbie; Métro: Iena.

Yves Saint Laurent: 5 Av Marceau; Métro: Alma-Marceau.

Jean-Louis Scherrer: 51 Av Montaigne; Métro: F.-D.-Roosevelt.

Emmanuel Ungaro: 2 Av Montaigne; Métro: F.-D.-Roosevelt.
Valentino: 17 bis Av Montaigne; Métro: F.-D.-Roosevelt.

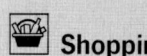
Shopping

(See also pages 40–42)

Articles de Paris and fashion accessories

Leather goods, perfume, soap, silk scarves, fashion jewellery and much more are available in Paris in fantastic abundance.
Bagagerie: 13 Rue Tronchet (Métro: Havre-Caumartin) and 41 Rue du Four (Métro: St-Germain-des-Prés).
Bingo: 3 Rue Scribe; Métro: Opéra.
Cambray: 8 Rue Pasquier; Métro: Madeleine.
Lucien Dalsace: 37 Bd St-Michel; Métro: St-Michel.
Christian Dior: 30 Av Montaigne; Métro: F.-D.-Roosevelt.
Eden Opéra: 212 Rue de Rivoli; Métro: Concorde.
Frany: Handbag specialists, 1 Rue de Sèvres; Métro: Sèvres-Babylone.
Fred: 6 Rue Royale; Métro: Concorde.
Guerlain: Perfume of this brand can be obtained only at the Guerlain shops at 2 Place Vendôme (Métro: Opéra) and 68 Champs-Elysées (Métro: F.-D.-Roosevelt).
Hermès: 24 Rue du Faubourg St-Honoré (Métro: Concorde) and in the Hilton Hotel, 18 Av de Suffren (Métro: Ecole Militaire).
Miss Paris: 20 Av de l'Opéra; Métro: Opéra.
Misukoschi: 49 Av de l'Opéra; Métro: Pyramides.
Nina Ricci: 22 Rue des Capucines (Métro: Opéra) and 17 Rue François Ier (Métro: F.-D. Roosevelt).
Rigaud: 51 Rue François Ier; Métro: George V.
Roger et Gallet: 62 Rue du Faubourg St-Honoré; Métro: Madeleine.

Prêt-à-porter — Ready-to-wear clothes

In addition to the ready-to-wear departments in the major department stores, the following shops also offer an interesting selection:
Actuel: 250 Rue St-Denis; Métro: Réaumur Sébastopol.
Balmain-Vendôme: 237 Rue St-Honoré; Métro: Tuileries.
Chloé Boutique: 3 Rue Gribeauval; Métro: Rue du Bac.
Chochotte Couture: 34 Rue St-André-des-Arts; Métro: Odéon.
Catherine Géraud Boutique: 58 bis Rue de la Chaussée d'Antin; Métro: Trinité.
Daniel Hechter Boutique: 146 Bd St-Germain; Métro: St-Germain-des-Prés.
Hit Parade: 35 Rue de la Chaussée d'Antin; Métro: Trinité.
Guy Laroche Boutique: 47 Rue de Rennes (Métro: St-Germain-des-Prés) and 30 Faubourg St-Honoré (Métro: Miromesnil).
Léonard Boutique: 234 Rue de Rivoli; Métro: Concorde.
Queenie: 10–12 Rue du Four; Métro: St-Germain-des-Prés.
Yves Saint Laurent Boutique: 90 Av des Champs-Elysées; Métro: George V.

Major department stores

Au Printemps: 64 Bd Haussmann; Métro: Havre-Caumartin.
Galeries Lafayette: 40 Bd Haussmann; Métro: Chaussée d'Antin.
Aux Trois Quartiers: 17 Bd de la Madeleine; Métro: Madeleine.

La Samaritaine: 75 Rue de Rivoli; Métro: Châtelet.
Bazar de l'Hôtel de Ville: 52 Rue de Rivoli; Métro: Hôtel de Ville.
Au Bon Marché: 20 Rue de Sèvres; Métro: Sèvres-Babylone.

Modern shopping centres

Forum des Halles: 1–7 Rue Pierre-Lescot; Métro: Les Halles.
Maine-Montparnasse: 17 Rue de l'Arrivée; Métro: Montparnasse.
Palais de Congrès at Porte Maillot (Air Terminal); Métro: Porte Maillot.
Les Quatre Temps: Parvis de la Défense (Hauts-de-Seine); Métro/RER: La Défense.

Shopping arcades

Old arcades, some newly discovered, in which attractive shops have been opened; ideal for a shopping trip in rainy weather.
Passage des Pavillons: Rue du Beaujolais (in the Palais Royal); Métro: Pyramides.
Galerie Vero-Dodat: 19 Rue J.-J. Rousseau; Métro: Louvre.
Passage du Caire: 2 Place du Caire; Métro: Sentier.
Passage Choiseul: Rue St-Augustin; Métro: Quatre-Septembre.
Passage des Princes: 97 Rue de Richelieu; Métro: Richelieu-Drouot.
Galerie Vivienne: Rue des Petits-Champs; Métro: Bourse.
Passage Jouffroy: 12 Bd Montmartre; Métro: Montmartre.
Passage Verdeau: 31 Rue du Faubourg Montmartre; Métro: Le Peletier.

Flea-markets and second-hand goods

Flea-market, *Marché aux Puces,* in St-Ouen at Porte de Clignancourt: Sat., Sun., Mon. 7 am–7.30 pm. Métro: Porte de Clignancourt.
Market at the Porte de Didot: Sat., Sun. 7 am–7.30 pm. Métro: Porte de Vanves.
Market in the Place d'Aligre: Every morning except Mon. Métro: Ledru-Rollin.
Market at the Porte de Montreuil: Sat. and Sun. Métro: Montreuil.

Specialist markets

Second-hand booksellers (Bouquinistes): on the Quai du Louvre and the Quai de la Mégisserie (Métro: Pont-Neuf), and on the Quai des Grands-Augustins, Quai de Conti and Quai de Malaquais (Métro: St-Michel).
Stamp and postcard market: In Av Gabriel, Thurs., Sat., Sun. from 10 am. Métro: Champs-Elysées-Clemenceau.
Flower market: In the Place Louis-Lépine and on the Quai de la Corse, Mon.–Sat. 8 am–7.30 pm. Métro: Cité.
Bird market: In the Place Louis-Lépine and on the Quai de la Corse, Sun. 8 am–7.30 pm. Métro: Cité.

Art and antiques markets

Le Louvre des Antiquaires in the Palais Royal: 250 dealers, an art market of world renown! Also interesting special exhibitions. Métro: Palais Royal.
Le Nouveau Drouot, 9 Rue Drouot: Paris auction room (11 am–noon and 2–6 pm). Métro: Richelieu-Drouot.
Antique-shops on the Left Bank within the square formed by the Quai Voltaire, Rue des Sts-Pères, Rue de l'Université and Rue du Bac, including the Rue de Beaune and the Rue de Lille.
La Cour aux Antiquaires, 54 Rue du Faubourg St-Honoré. Métro: Concorde.
Le Village St-Paul: Rue St-Paul, Rue des Jardins St-Paul, Rue de l'Ave Maria, Quai des Célestins. Métro: Sully-Morland.

Paris stamp market

Books

The large bookshops on the Left Bank (Bd St-Michel, Bd St-Germain) stock everything – you have only to look for it. Book supermarkets: *FNAC-Forum* (Forum des Halles; Métro: Les Halles) and *FNAC-Montparnasse* (136 Rue de Rennes; Métro: Rennes/St-Placide).
Art bookshop: *Artcurial*, 9 Av Matignon; Métro: F.-D.-Roosevelt.

Delicatessens

The high-class, and expensive, establishments are concentrated around the Place de la Madeleine. The great attractions for gourmets include *Fauchon*, the most famous delicatessen in the city (no. 26), the truffle specialist *Maison de la Truffe* (no. 19), *Hédiard*, with its exotic delicacies (no. 21) and many others.
Foie gras: Relatively good value for money at *Boucherie Bernard*, 19 Rue Danielle-Casanova (Métro: Pyramides); there are another dozen Bernard branches scattered around Paris.
Caviare: *Petrossian*, Bd Latour-Maubourg (Métro: Latour-Maubourg), with the largest selection in Paris.
Cheese: *Androuet*, the 'high priest of cheese', not only of Paris but also worldwide (see page 42), 41 Rue d'Amsterdam (Métro: Liège); *La Ferme St-Hubert*, 21 Rue Vignon (Métro: Madeleine); *Creplet-Brussol*, 17 Place de la Madeleine (Métro: Madeleine).
Wines and spirits: There are cellars with fine selections of wines and spirits all over the city. You will be offered competent assistance by virtually all wine dealers. For this reason, only three selections are given here:
Jean Danflou: Tasting room for the finest high-proof spirits. 36 Rue du Mont-Thabor; Métro: Concorde.
La Galerie des Vins: The mecca for devotees of red Bordeaux! 201 Rue St-Honoré; Métro: Palais Royal.
Petrissans: Specialists in the wines of Burgundy and Bordeaux. Tasting room. 30 bis Av Niel; Métro: Ternes.
Do not forget the various street markets, where it is possible to find first-class products at reasonable prices. Every district of the city has its food market. The largest and best-known are:
Marché de la Mouffe: Rue Mouffetard; Métro: Monge.
Marché de la Rue de Buci; Métro: Odéon.
Marché de la Rue Lepic; Métro: Blanche (only Tues. and Fri., 7 am – 1 pm).

Select items for the home

Christofle: All kinds of silverware for the table. 12 Rue Royale; Métro: Madeleine.
Arlequin: Large selection of old glasses. 13 Rue des Francs-Bourgeois; Métro: St-Paul.
Lalique: The 1920s glasses now fashionable again are still produced here. 11 Rue Royale; Métro: Concorde.
Habitat France: Large selection of beautiful, original items for the home. Forum des Halles, 1 Rue Pierre-Lescot; Métro: Les Halles.

Culinarion: Kitchen equipment for every need. 99 Rue de Rennes; Métro: St-Sulpice.

Vangal: Art Deco and other styles of lamps and lampshades. Antique and reproduction. 87 Rue St-Denis; Métro: Réaumur-Sébastopol.

Records

Discophile Club de France, 6 Rue Monsieur-le-Prince; Métro: Odéon.
FNAC, 142 Rue de Rennes; Métro: St-Placide.
FNAC, Forum des Halles; Métro: Les Halles.
Lido-Musique, 68 Champs-Elysées; Métro: F.-D.-Roosevelt.

Jewellery

The most celebrated jewellers are concentrated around the Place Vendôme and the adjoining streets: Van Cleef & Arpels, Boucheron, Cartier, Bulgari and others. Two special establishments are selected here.

Clerc: A wide choice of jewels and expensive watches. A particularly beautiful shop in the *Directoire* style. 4 Place de l'Opéra; Métro: Opéra.

Espace Bijoux: Sells the previous season's haute-couture jewellery at reduced prices. 2 Galerie Vivienne; Métro: Bourse.

Lingerie

The most diaphanous creations will be found at:
Frivolités – Au bon choix, 56 Bd de Clichy; Métro: Blanche.
Cadolle, 14 Rue Cambon; Métro: Concorde.
Candide, 4 Rue de Miromesnil; Métro: Miromesnil.
Cashmere House, 2 Rue d'Aguesseau; Métro: Madeleine.

Beyond the city – selected excursions

For many hundreds of years, Paris has been the centre of the *Île-de-France*, the historical and cultural heartland of France. In comparison with many other cities, Paris has expanded far beyond its official boundaries. Many places in the near suburbs (*proche banlieue*) have been almost imperceptibly swallowed up by the great metropolis. Thus visitors to *St-Denis* – which is in fact a separate town with a population of 100,000 – will scarcely notice that they are actually quite a long way outside Paris.

The whole conurbation, which since 1964 has been incorporated into a single entity known as the *Région Parisienne*, covers approximately 1,100 sq km, and extends deep into the surrounding area, not always to the latter's advantage. The pull of the metropolis has led irresistibly to the urbanisation of the suburbs, the *banlieue*. This only serves to make even more precious those parks and forests around Paris that have so far withstood the pressures of development: the Bois de Boulogne and the Bois de Vincennes, the grounds of châteaux such as *Versailles, St-Germain* and *Rambouillet*, and the romantic forest of Fontainebleau.

For 1,000 years, the relationship between Paris and its surrounding area has been one of creative tension, in which both have been equal partners. The Île-de-France was the birthplace of Gothic architecture: from *St-Denis*, the glorious road leads to *Chartres* and *Notre-Dame, Mantes* and *Senlis, Beauvais* and the *Sainte-Chapelle*. The same process occurs with the châteaux: François I was building at the Louvre and in Fontainebleau at the same time, while Louis XIV left Paris in order to build Versailles in the image of Vaux-le-

Beyond the city – selected excursions

Vicomte. It was not until the 19th c. that Paris gained a clear advantage over its surrounding area. Could it be that today the trend is beginning to be reversed? Massive construction projects, such as *La Défense*, are already thrusting into the sky of the Île-de-France on the edge of the city.

Versailles

Whenever Versailles is mentioned, virtually everybody thinks of the palace rather than the town, which has 100,000 inhabitants but otherwise nothing of real note. But then whenever the talk is of the palace which has made Versailles famous throughout the world, the figure of Louis XIV, the Sun King, inevitably looms large. He is the embodiment of 17th c. absolutism, a doctrine which enabled him to declare, unabashed and without fear of contradiction: 'L'état, c'est moi!' The architectural symbol of this overweening sense of power and self-confidence is the Palace of Versailles.

Most visitors to the palace are in fact less impressed by its beauty than by its sheer immensity. This was also the case during the period of its construction, from 1661 to 1710: the works involved no fewer than 36,000 people (and 6,000 horses) and were directed by the most celebrated architects in France: Louis Le Vau, Jules Hardouin-Mansart and Robert de Cotte. Charles Le Brun was responsible for the interior, while André Le Nôtre laid out the gardens. The palace façade is 680 m long. In Louis XIV's time there were around 20,000 people at the royal court: 1,000 members of the nobility and their 4,000 servants occupied hundreds of rooms in the palace itself, a further 5,000 servants were accommodated in the outlying buildings and about 10,000 soldiers were billeted in the town. Even then Versailles was said to be 'the most magnificent palace of all time'. As the centre of world political power it was above all widely feared, but naturally also opposed.

The authority that the building represents can almost be sensed physically as one approaches the palace – and this was precisely the impression it was intended to create. The visitor walks across the *Place d'Armes*, the point of convergence of three wide avenues which lead up to the magnificent entrance and are bounded by the former royal stables. He then goes through a splendid gateway, with the original

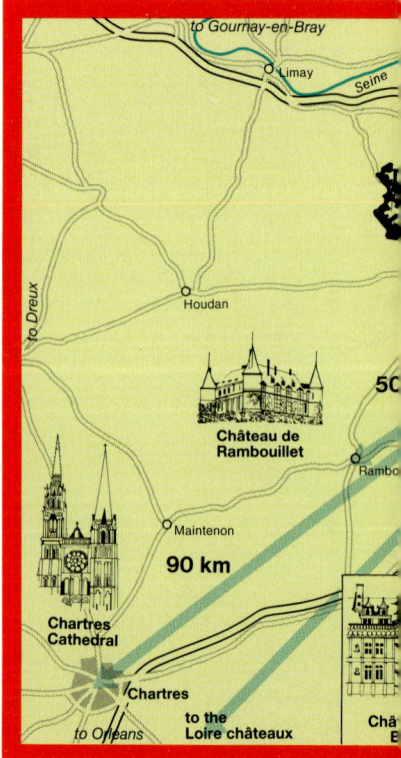

Beyond the city – selected excursions

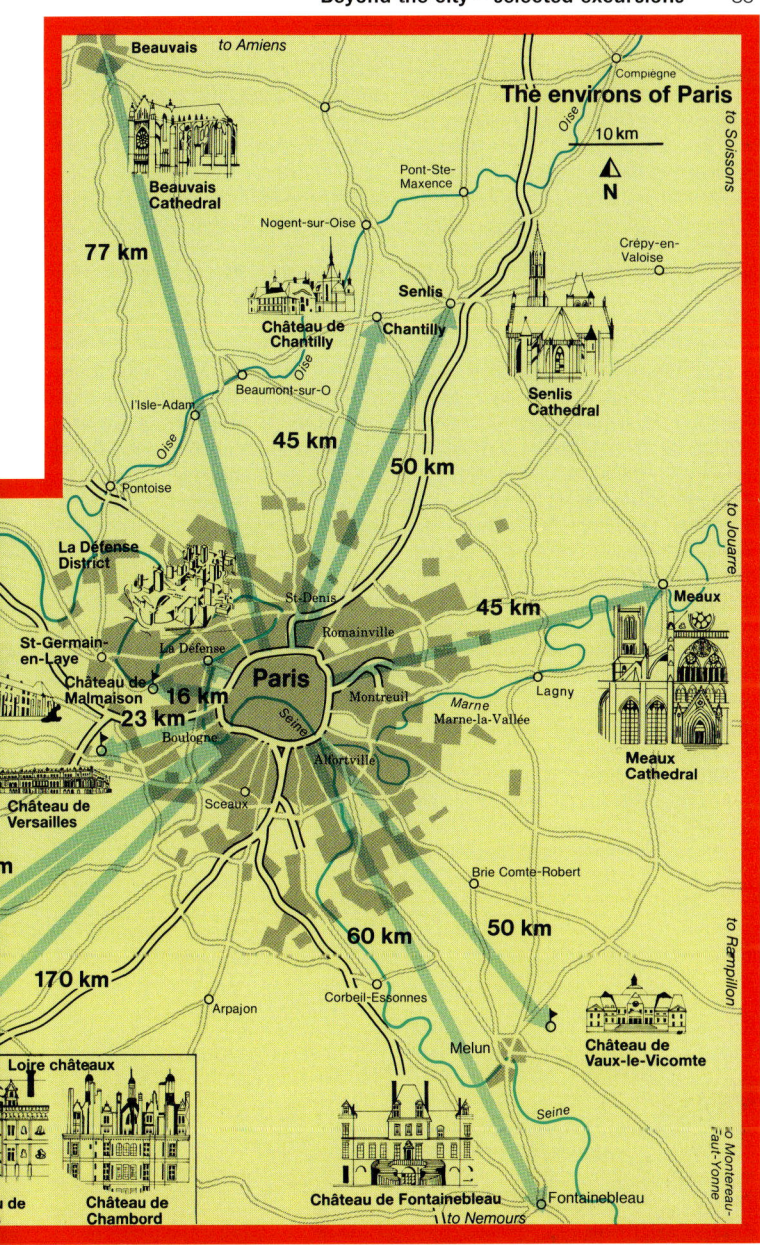

grille, walks past the equestrian statue of Louis XIV and across the cobblestones of the *Cour Royale* and finally, at the far side of the *Cour de Marbre*, reaches the palace gates.

For your visit to the palace, it is advisable to join one of the guided tours (also available in English). Nevertheless, it is an exhausting march through the seemingly endless corridors, with their apartments, salons, chambers and antechambers, in which there is indeed a great deal to see, but very little of great significance. One undoubted exception is the *Galerie des Glaces* (Hall of Mirrors), 75 m long and 10 m wide; even by the standards of Versailles, it is extraordinarily splendid. It was here, on June 28th 1919, that the Treaty of Versailles was signed, which brought an end to the First World War. Also of particular interest are the chapel (a major work by Hardouin-Mansart), in which Louis XVI and Marie-Antoinette were married, the *Salon d'Hercule*, with the massive ceiling-painting known as the 'Apotheosis of Hercules', and several of the royal apartments.

After the long trek through the suites of rooms, a breath of fresh air in the gardens will be very welcome – and deserved. Extending over an area of about 100 ha, the gardens of Versailles are quite simply the masterpiece of French garden design. They were created by Le Nôtre, who also laid out the Tuileries. His overriding purpose was to subject nature to the laws of geometry and symmetry. No tree was to grow as it wished, no water was to follow its natural course. The resolute will of the creator can be best observed by walking along the main axis of the garden, from the terrace via the *Parterres d'Eau* and the *Tapis Vert* to the *Bassin d'Apollon* and the beginning of the *Grand Canal*. It is from here also that the imposing grandeur of the palace façade is seen to best advantage.

From the Grand Canal an avenue on the right leads to the *Trianons*. The *Grand Trianon* was built in 1687 by Hardouin-Mansart for Louis XIV and his mistress Madame de Maintenon. The charming *Allée du Mail* leads through the formal gardens of the Trianon. The *Petit Trianon* was built eighty years later by the Sun King's great-grandson, Louis XV, for his mistress Madame de Pompadour. The relative intimacy of this French Rococo building and its well-preserved Louis XV furniture is perhaps more appealing to us today than the somewhat remote splendour of the

Versailles

grand siècle, the classical period of Louis XIV. In later years the Petit Trianon became Marie-Antoinette's refuge from the etiquette of the royal court, which she found such a burden. The naïve romanticism that so inspired the unfortunate wife of the unfortunate King Louis XVI is reflected most particularly in the *Hameau*, a sort of imitation village, complete with farm buildings, dairy, mill and dovecot, which she had built as a setting for her pastoral make-believe, until the outbreak of the Revolution jolted her out of her ingenuous dreams. The Petit Trianon and the Hameau stand in a part of the park laid out in the then popular English style, which provides a most welcome relief from the formal rigour of French landscape gardening. Not least for this reason, you should really set aside a whole day for your visit to Versailles.

How to get there: By car from the Porte de St-Cloud on the A13, 23 km (car-park in the Place d'Armes); by RER, line C5, 15 minutes to Versailles Rive-Gauche.

Opening times: Palace: daily except Mon. and public holidays 10 am–5 pm; Grand and Petit Trianons: daily except Tues. 2–5.30 pm in summer, 2–5 pm in winter. The gardens and park are open from dawn to dusk.

The fountains are operational on the first and third Sundays of the months May–September between 4.30 and 6 pm.

Malmaison

The Château de Malmaison, which lies in a loop of the Seine west of Paris, preserves memories of what were probably the happiest days in the life of Napoleon I. The palace, built at the beginning of the 17th c., was acquired in 1799 by Josephine Bonaparte, the widow of the Vicomte de Beauharnais. She had the two side wings built. It was here, in the company of his capricious wife, that Napoleon, who as First Consul and then as Emperor resided in the Tuileries, spent the few precious hours away from the constraints of etiquette that his military and governmental duties allowed him. Josephine excelled at holding sumptuous gatherings, at which the company was decidedly mixed; these sometimes took place during her husband's absence, which naturally gave rise to repeated quarrels.

Even after Napoleon had divorced her – for dynastic reasons – Josephine continued to live at Malmaison, of which she had become very fond, until her death in May 1814. Today the château houses a museum dedicated to the memory of Napoleon and Josephine. Part of the splendid original furnishings can still be seen, for example in the music room, the dining room, the council chamber, the library and Josephine's apartments.

How to get there: By car from Porte Maillot and via La Défense and Nanterre to Rueil-Malmaison, 16 km; by RER, line A1, from Opéra or Etoile via La Défense to Rueil-Malmaison.

Museum opening times: Daily except Tues. 10 am–noon and 1.30–5.30 pm in summer, until 4.30 pm in winter.

St-Germain-en-Laye

The château is in the east of the pretty, almost elegant residential suburb which lies on a plateau overlooking the Seine. The old castle, built in the 12th c., was at various times damaged, partly demolished, converted and extended. Of the oldest parts of the castle, the chapel has fortunately survived; it was built by Louis IX between 1230 and 1238 and is often seen as a precursor of the Sainte-Chapelle in Paris.

Also of note is the *Salle de Mars*, built during the reign of François I, once the royal guardroom and later a ballroom, in which lavish celebrations and dramatic performances were held during the reign of Louis XIV. Henri II, Charles IX and Louis XIV were born at St-Germain. During the reign of Henri IV his fourteen children, legitimate and illegitimate alike, lived in the royal apartments on the first floor.

The extensive gardens are particularly beautiful; they were originally laid out by Le Nôtre and completed in 1673. Today there are sections in both the English and the French styles. The *Petite Terrasse* begins at the *Pavillon-Henri-IV* and stretches as far as the *Rond-Point du Rosarium*, where there is an orientation table. The *Grande Terrasse* continues for a further 2.4 km, bordered all the way by old lime trees. This is a delightful walk, for the sake of which you should, if necessary, cut short your visit to the château.

How to get there: By car from Porte Maillot via La Défense and Nanterre on Route Nationale 190, 20 km; by RER, line A1, from Opéra or Etoile via La Défense to St-Germain-en-Laye.

Opening times: Daily except Tues. 9.45 am–noon and 1.30–5.15 pm. All visitors to the chapel must be accompanied by a guide. It is worth combining a visit to St-Germain-en-Laye with a trip to Malmaison.

Fontainebleau

The palace owes its existence to two royal passions: hunting and women. Its first great period was in the 16th c., when François I had the medieval castle torn down and a modern palace built for his mistress, the Duchess of Etampes. He assembled a group of celebrated Italian artists, who brought 'their' Renaissance style with them to France. This so-called Fontainebleau School was the starting point of the French Renaissance. The palace itself offers a good visual lesson in the development of the new architectural language. The memory of Diane de Poitiers, the favourite of Henri II and one of the famous women of French history, also lives on in Fontainebleau.

In the centuries that followed, several monarchs made further additions to the palace. Louis XIII was born here, Louis XIV signed the revocation of the Edict of Nantes in the palace and Louis XV was married here. However, it was Napoleon who next put the stamp of his era on the palace. The Emperor resided in Fon-

The Château de Malmaison

tainebleau when he had had enough of the cold splendour of the Tuileries (at these times he spoke of *la tristesse de la grandeur*), although it was here in April 1814 that he had to sign the act of abdication. Prior to that, Pope Pius VII had spent two years in the palace as a prisoner of the French. The finest rooms in the palace include the *Galerie François I* (1528–44), a masterpiece of Early Renaissance decoration, the *Galerie Henri II* (c. 1550) with symbolic emblems of Diane de Poitiers, the *Salon Louis XIII*, in which that king was born in 1601, and the *Galerie des Assiettes*, decorated with Sèvres plates painted with views of French royal palaces. Other parts of the palace in the Empire style are a reflection of the Napoleonic period.

The palace is situated in beautiful gardens: the *Jardin de Diane* to the north, the *Parterre*, laid out by Le Nôtre for Louis XIV, with its sculptures and ornamental ponds, and the *Jardin Anglais*, laid out for Napoleon. The nearby Forest of Fontainebleau, the former hunting ground of kings, with its ravines and magnificent ancient trees, is still, in part at least, an extremely picturesque area.

How to get there: By car from Paris on the A6 (Autoroute du Sud), 60 km; by train from the Gare de Lyon (bus from Fontainebleau station or 30 minutes on foot).

Opening times: Daily except Tues. 10 am–noon and 1–5 pm, in winter until 4 pm.

Other châteaux

Chantilly: A beautiful château, consisting of two connected buildings, one Renaissance and one Baroque; 'French garden' by Le Nôtre, and the Musée Condé with the famous book of hours *Les très riches heures du duc de Berri*. Daily except Tues. 10.30 am–5 pm. 45 km north of Paris.

Rambouillet: 18th c. château with particularly splendid park (hermitage, sheep-farm). Marble Room, Marie-Antoinette's boudoir and bathroom with beautiful Delft tiles. Summer home of the French president, open to the public only when he is not in residence. Daily 10 am–noon and 2–6 pm, in winter until 4 pm. 50 km south-west of Paris.

Sceaux: Château with beautiful park (Le Nôtre), fountains, concerts and flower shows. 12 km south. Suburban line from the Gare du Luxembourg, or Châtelet.

Vaux-le-Vicomte: The château and park dating from around 1650 served as Louis XIV's models for Versailles. Certainly worth a visit. 50 km south of Paris. Château and gardens open only on Sat. and Sun.

The Loire châteaux: A trip to the Loire can be included in a visit to Paris. (See the RAC Travel Guide *France: Loire Valley*.)

Cathedrals

For lovers of Gothic cathedrals, the environs of Paris offer much of interest. Of the cathedrals in the Île-de-France, *Chartres* (90 km south-west of Paris) and *Beauvais* (77 km to the north), which was never finished, are particularly worth seeing. A visit to Chartres can be included in an excursion to Versailles or Rambouillet. Less well known but also very impressive are the cathedrals of *Meaux* (45 km east) and *Senlis* (50 km north-east).

All the excursions mentioned above can be booked through the major tour operators in Paris.

Useful things to know

Climate, time to visit

Paris has a temperate climate: mild winters with little snow, and tolerable heat in summer. It is a city for all seasons. It is perhaps at its most beautiful in April, but the long, warm evenings of May and June can also be enchanting. The unique silvery, shimmering light of the Île-de-France is seen to best advantage in autumn, when the city is full of activity and *joie de vivre*. In winter, when the theatre, concert and social seasons are in full swing, Paris shows its most cultivated side. Only in August is Paris boring. The Parisians are on holiday, most of the shops are closed and the tourists have the place to themselves.

Passport and customs regulations

No visa required by British or US visitors staying under three months. British tourists need a valid standard passport or British Visitor's Passport.

Personal belongings of people entering the country are not subject to duty. These include still and video cameras, tape recorders, portable radios, telescopes and binoculars, portable typewriters and the usual camping equipment. In addition, EC residents may bring in (duty paid) 300 cigarettes (or 75 cigars or 400 g tobacco), 5 litres of wine and 1.5 litres of spirits over 22% (3 litres under 22%).

EC residents may take into or bring back from France duty free 200 cigarettes or 50 cigars or 250 g tobacco, 1 litre of spirits over 22% (2 litres under 22%) and 2 litres of wine.

Non-EC visitors should check allowances with their travel agents.

Insurance

You are strongly advised to take out holiday insurance, including cover against medical expenses.

As a member of the EC France has a reciprocal agreement with other EC countries, under which free medical treatment can be obtained for those entitled to it in their own country. To obtain this benefit a UK national has to be in possession of form E111, obtainable from the DSS; an application form is available from the DSS or at main post offices.

Anyone travelling by car should arrange comprehensive insurance cover for the duration of the holiday.

Money: currency and exchange

The unit of currency is the franc (F), divided into 100 centimes (c). Exchange rates are subject to fluctuation and should be checked at a bank or via the national press. Import restrictions and exchange controls are of no practical significance for tourists.

Those wanting to change foreign currency will usually require their passports. The use of credit cards has increased in recent years. However, in the numerous family-run establishments (small hotels, restaurants and shops) that still fortunately exist in France, the rule is often that 'on n'accepte pas les chèques'. This refers to cheques and credit cards alike. It is a good idea, therefore, to carry an adequate supply of cash with you.

Most banks are open Monday to Friday from 9 am to 4.30 pm. On Sundays, tourists can change money in the Office de Tourisme (127 Champs-Elysées, 9 am–10 pm), at major railway stations and at airports.

Arriving by car

The only papers required are your car registration documents and driving licence. A 'green card' (international insurance document) is no longer obligatory, but may be very useful in the event of an accident.

The main approach routes to Paris from the UK are the A13 from the northwest (joined by those arriving at Le Havre or Dieppe) and the A1 from the north (joined by those arriving at Calais, Boulogne or Dunkirk).

Arriving by air

There are direct flights to Paris from all major airports worldwide.

International flights arrive at Paris-Orly and Roissy-Charles-de-Gaulle. Regular bus services (every 15 minutes during busy periods) connect both airports with the terminals at Invalides (Métro: Invalides) and Porte Maillot (Métro: Porte Maillot). Given the frequent traffic jams, it is not much quicker to go by taxi and the cost is about three times greater.

Arriving by train

Trains from the northern Channel ports arrive at the Gare du Nord, while those from the north-western ports arrive at the Gare St-Lazare. Still a comfortable way of travelling to Paris.

Traffic

In theory, the same rules of the road prevail as in most other parts of Continental Europe. Exceptions: the maximum speed in Paris is 60 kph (37.5 mph), and traffic coming from the right almost always has priority (pay attention to all relevant signs). Drivers do not generally signal their intention to change lanes. The law of the stronger and quicker is applied fairly unscrupulously. Little special consideration is accorded to foreigners or strangers to Paris. The police do not concern themselves with the very frequent collisions, provided it is only cars that sustain damage. The parking situation in central Paris ranges from difficult to catastrophic. The upshot of all this is that you would be well advised to use public transport (see under Buses, Métro and Taxis).

Buses

Bus stops are indicated by circular yellow and red signs, marked with the route number and name of the stop. All are request stops: you must signal to the driver. When you want to get off, ring the bell. If you are going to use the buses frequently, it makes sense to buy a *carnet*, or book of ten tickets. These can be obtained at all Métro stations as they are also valid for the Métro.

Boat trips on the Seine: A highly recommended excursion, which lasts either 1½ or 2½ hours. The most famous company is 'Les Bateaux-Mouches'. Departures every day between 10 am and 10 pm in summer, and between 11 am and 4 pm in winter, from *Port de la Conférence* on the Right Bank, between the Pont des Invalides and the Pont de l'Alma. For information, tel. 42 25 96 10.

Métro

Originally known officially as the *Chemin de fer métropolitain*. Although it was opened in 1900, the Paris Métro has the densest and most readily comprehensible network of any comparable metropolis in the world; it is the cheapest, quickest and hence most popular means of transport for Parisians. Even strangers to the city will find their way about without difficulty with the aid of the maps in the Métro stations and the schematic diagrams of each line to be found in all carriages. The total length of the network is approximately 186 km (116 miles), while the individual stations are only 500 m apart. Thus virtually any point in Paris can be reached easily by Métro. The trains run from 5.30 am to 1.15 am at intervals of between one and eight minutes.

You can buy tickets in a book of ten (*un carnet*). There are also several convenient passes: *Formule 1* allows unrestricted use of the Métro, RER (regional service) and bus for one day; *Carte Orange* (photo required) allows you to do the same for a week, from Monday to Sunday, and is especially good value; finally, there are 2-, 4- and 7-day tourist tickets (*billet de tourisme* or *Paris-Sésame*) that are valid on the Métro and several of the RER lines. The RER lines will take you quickly and comfortably to the outlying districts of Paris. Maps of the Métro are available free of charge from all Métro stations.

Taxis

Paris taxis suffer from an international disease: when you don't need one, there are hundreds available; if you need one urgently (at a station, in pouring rain or to get to the theatre on time), there is never one to be seen. If you want to make sure of getting one, you should order a Radio-Taxi by telephoning one of the following numbers: 47 39 33 33, 42 03 99 99, 42 05 77 77 or 42 70 41 41. Fares are shown on the meter and are on average lower than in many European countries. They are increased for journeys between 10 pm and 6.30 am, and supplements are charged for journeys to and from railway stations and air terminals. Each piece of luggage is subject to an additional charge. A tip of at least 10% of the fare is expected.

Parking

A virtually insoluble problem! In the short-term parking zones – *zones bleues* – the maximum stay is only 90 minutes, except on Sundays and public holidays. These zones are indicated by a blue circle on the lamp posts. In side-streets, parking is permitted on the odd-numbered side during the first half of the month, and on the even-numbered side in the second half. Parking is forbidden in the areas indicated by yellow and red stripes on the kerb, 15 m either side of bus stops, in front of schools and monuments and in many other places that are nevertheless packed with cars, and which can be recognised only by the traffic wardens diligently taking numbers. Their regulations make no provision for preferential treatment for foreigners. The only real chance of finding a parking space is in the underground public car-parks.

Sightseeing tours of the city

A number of companies offer sightseeing tours of the city, with only minimal differences in programme and price. The largest are: *Cityrama*, Place des Pyramides; *Havas Voyages*, 26 Av de l'Opéra; *Paris Excursions*, 1 Rue Auber. It is most convenient to book through your hotel, where you will also find the relevant brochures. It may be a good idea to use a tour of all the main sights as a means of orientating yourself in the city. However, do not join a tour whose programme includes a visit to the Louvre. You will not have the time to do the museum justice.

There are two ways of seeing 'Paris by night'. The first is a tour of the city's illuminated buildings and monuments, and includes a son et lumière entertainment at the Dôme des Invalides. The second is an introduction to Paris nightlife, with visits to music halls, cabarets and nightclubs. There are also tours offering combinations of these two areas of interest.

The same companies also offer excursions to various destinations within easy reach of Paris, e.g. Versailles,

Malmaison, Fontainebleau or the châteaux of the Loire.

Police
Paris police officers – colloquially *flics* or (more vulgarly) *vaches* – are generally very polite, but noticeably impatient with drivers who, not knowing how to drive in Paris, impede the swift flow of the traffic, often because they are observing the speed limit.

Each arrondissement has its own *commissariat de police*, where thefts should be reported and where the addresses of doctors and pharmacists with a night-time or Sunday service are also held. The *Préfecture de Police* (headquarters) is on the Île de la Cité at 9 Bd du Palais; Métro: Cité.

Youth hostels
Since the city is always crowded, it is advisable to book in advance. Reservations can also be made through the Office de Tourisme (see page 93).
Auberge de Jeunesse de Paris: 8 Bd Jules Ferry, tel. 43 57 55 60; Métro: République. *Auberge de Jeunesse,* 14 Rue de Trévise, tel. 47 70 90 94; Métro: Montmartre. *Auberge de Jeunesse,* 12 Rue des Barres, tel. 42 72 72 09; Métro: Hôtel de Ville. Student hall of residence *Union des Maisons d'Etudiants* (UME), 93 Bd St-Michel, tel. 46 34 11 16; Métro: Luxembourg.

Camping
The Paris campsite is in the Bois de Boulogne on the banks of the Seine, Route du Bord-de-l'Eau; Métro: Porte Maillot (bus link). Tel. 45 24 30 00. Information on other campsites in the Paris region from the Office de Tourisme (see page 93).

Public holidays
January 1st, Easter Monday, May 1st (Labour Day), Ascension Day, Whit Monday, July 14th (Fête Nationale, or Bastille Day), August 15th (Assumption), November 1st (All Saints' Day), November 11th (Armistice Day) and December 25th.

Calendar of events
January: 'Prix d'Amérique' horse-race at the Vincennes racecourse.
March: Salon des Arts Ménagers (home economics, home furnishings and décor) in the Palais du CNIT at the Rond-Point de la Défense; Foire au Jambon ('Ham Market'), Bd Richard-Lenoir.
April: Displays of tulips, hyacinths and azaleas in the Parc Bagatelle (Bois de Boulogne) and in the Botanical Gardens in the Bois de Vincennes; Foire du Trône (Throne Fair, or carnival) in the Bois de Vincennes.
May: Salon International de l'Aéronautique et de l'Espace (Paris Air Show), Le Bourget airport (every two years); international festival of drama at the Châtelet; Foire de Paris (Paris Show) at the Parc des Expositions, Porte de Versailles.
June: International tennis championships at the Stade Roland-Garros; international horse-races at Auteuil, Longchamp and St-Cloud.
June/July: Festival of music and drama in the Marais; roses in bloom in the Parc Bagatelle and the Botanical Gardens.
July: July 14th (Bastille Day): military parade along the Champs-Elysées, and fairs and celebrations in various localities; Tour de France cycle race ends in Paris.
July/August: Festival estival (summer festival) on the Île de la Cité and in the Latin Quarter.
September: The fountains play at St-Cloud; dahlias in bloom in the Botanical Gardens; Salon du Meuble (furniture exhibition), Rue du Faubourg St-Antoine; Semaine Internationale du Cuir (inter-

national leather fair) at the Parc des Expositions, Porte de Versailles.
October: Fête des Vendanges (grape-harvest festival), Montmartre; 'Grand Prix de l'Arc de Triomphe' horse-race on the first Sunday in October at Longchamp; Salon d'Automne (Autumn Art Exhibition) in the Grand Palais; Salon de l'Automobile (Motor Show) in the Parc des Expositions, Porte de Versailles.
November: International festival of dance at the Théâtre des Champs-Elysées; military parade on November 11th along the Champs-Elysées, on the anniversary of Armistice Day 1918.

Programmes of events

These are to be found in the magazines *Pariscope – une semaine de Paris* and *L'Officiel des spectacles*, which are published every Wednesday and are available at all newspaper kiosks.

Son et lumière

Entertainment staged at night in or against the backdrop of a historical monument, usually a palace, whereby the history of the location is 'brought to life' by means of lighting effects, sound effects and narration. In Paris such spectacles are held at the Dôme des Invalides and the Château de Vincennes; also at Versailles (see under Sightseeing tours, page 90).

Telephones

The French telephone system has been modernised in recent years, and making a telephone call is no longer the frustrating experience it once was. Coin-operated telephones are becoming less common. All public telephones will soon be converted to accept *télécartes*, or phone cards, which are on sale in units of 40 or 120 in post offices and *tabacs*. The use of these cards cuts the cost of telephoning, since each unit is charged at less than the 1 F used in coin-operated telephones.

When calling abroad dial 19, wait for the tone, and then dial the code for the country you wish to call (44 for the UK, 1 for the US/Canada; omit initial 0 from area code).

Post and post offices

Post office opening times: Mon. to Fri. 8 am–7 pm, Sat. 8 am–noon. The central post office (Bureau de Poste Principal, 52 Rue du Louvre, tel. 40 28 20 00) is also open at night for making telephone calls and sending telegrams. Stamps (*timbres*) are sold not only in post offices but also in *bars tabacs* (bars with tobacco licence).

Swimming pools

The largest outdoor swimming pool in the city centre is the *Piscine Deligny*, Quai Anatole-France, Métro: Chambre des Députés.

If you are staying in Paris for a fairly long time, it is worth obtaining the complete list of pools and other sports facilities, available free of charge from the *Hall d'Accueil de la Ville de Paris*, 29 Rue de Rivoli, Métro: Hôtel de Ville.

Toilets

French toilets in their traditional form, which are now rapidly disappearing, have long been a part of travellers' folklore. However, those wanting to be certain that they will not have to stand rather than sit, and that proper paper will be available, often seek out a first-class hotel, whether they are staying there or not! An increasing number of modern, coin-operated 'super-loos' have recently been installed in the streets of Paris; in the wake of sexual equality, they have replaced the photogenic '*pissoirs*', the green-painted urinals that were once a great Paris institution.

Tobacco, cigarettes
In the city centre there are specialist shops selling tobacco, cigarettes, etc. However, it is normal practice to purchase one's requirements in the numerous bars with cigarette kiosks attached. Look for the red 'double cone' sign.

Shop opening hours
The official opening hours, observed only by larger shops and department stores, are from 9.30 am to 6 pm. Larger stores are usually closed on Mondays. Many food shops are open until 8 pm and on Sunday mornings.

Tipping
12–15% is usually included in restaurant and café bills. Usherettes in theatres and cinemas expect between 2 and 3 F.

Newspapers
English-language newspapers can be obtained around the Opéra, on the Champs-Elysées and in the Latin Quarter, usually on the day of publication.

Important addresses
Embassies
British Embassy
35 Rue du Faubourg St-Honoré
tel. 42 66 91 42

US Embassy
2 Av Gabriel
tel. 42 96 12 02

Canadian Embassy
35 Av Montaigne
tel. 47 23 01 01

Australian Embassy
4 Rue Jean Rey
tel. 45 75 62 00

New Zealand Embassy
7 ter Rue Léonard de Vinci
tel. 45 00 24 11

Irish Embassy
4 Rue Rude
tel. 45 00 20 87

Tourist information
In UK
French Government Tourist Office
178 Piccadilly
London W1V OAL
tel. 071 499 6911

In USA
French Government Tourist Office
610 Fifth Avenue
New York NYC 10021

In France
The *Office de Tourisme* (Bureau d'Accueil Central) is at 127 Av des Champs-Elysées, tel. 47 23 61 72 (daily 9 am–10 pm). Branches at the Gare du Nord, Gare d'Austerlitz, Gare de Lyon, Gare de l'Est and the Eiffel Tower. In addition, there is also a municipal tourist information office: Accueil de la Ville de Paris, 29 Rue de Rivoli, tel. 42 76 40 40.

Other important addresses
Emergency medical service: SOS Médecin, tel. 43 37 77 77 or 47 07 77 77.
Emergency dental service: SOS Dentiste, tel. 43 37 51 00.
Pharmacies: Pharmacie des Champs, 84 Av des Champs-Elysées, tel. 45 62 02 41 (24-hour service); Pharmacie Opéra, 6 Bd des Capucines, tel. 42 65 88 29 (night service); Pharmacie d'Italie, 61 Av d'Italie, tel. 43 31 19 72 (night service). The addresses of the nearest doctor and of a hospital with an ambulance service will be found in pharmacies, which are identified by a green cross on a white background.
Lost-property office (Bureau des objets trouvés): 36 Rue des Morillons (15e); Mon. Fri. 8.30 am–5 pm, Thurs. until 8 pm; tel. 48 28 20 00.
Emergency services: Police, tel. 17; Fire, tel. 18; First aid, emergency medical service (SAMU), tel. 45 67 50 50.

Useful words and phrases

Although English is fairly widely understood in Paris, the visitor will undoubtedly find a few words and phrases of French very useful.

please	s'il vous plaît
thank you (very much)	merci (bien)
yes/no	oui/non
excuse me	pardon
do you speak English?	parlez-vous anglais?
I do not understand	je ne comprends pas
good morning	bonjour
good evening	bonsoir
good night	bonne nuit
goodbye	au revoir
how much?	combien?
I should like	je voudrais
a room with private bath	une chambre avec bain
the bill, please! (in hotel)	la note, s'il vous plaît
(in restaurant)	l'addition
everything included	tout compris
when?	à quelle heure?
open	ouvert
shut	fermé
where is . . . street?	où se trouve la rue . . . ?
the road to?	la route de . . . ?
how far is it to . . . ?	quelle est la distance à . . . ?
to the left/right	à gauche/à droite
straight on	tout droit
post office	le bureau de poste
railway station	la gare
town hall	l'hôtel de ville/la mairie
exchange office	le bureau de change
police station	le commissariat/la poste de police
public telephone	la cabine téléphonique
tourist information office	l'office de tourisme/ le syndicat d'initiative
doctor	le médecin
chemist	le pharmacien
toilet	la toilette
ladies	dames
gentlemen	messieurs
engaged	occupé
free	libre
entrance	l'entrée
exit	la sortie
today/tomorrow	aujourd'hui/demain
Sunday/Monday	dimanche/lundi
Tuesday/Wednesday	mardi/mercredi
Thursday/Friday	jeudi/vendredi
Saturday/holiday	samedi/jeu de congé

- 0 zéro
- 1 un/une
- 2 deux
- 3 trois
- 4 quatre
- 5 cinq
- 6 six
- 7 sept
- 8 huit
- 9 neuf
- 10 dix
- 11 onze
- 12 douze
- 20 vingt
- 50 cinquante
- 100 cent

Index

Arc de Triomphe 51, 65
Arc de Triomphe du Carrousel 49, 65
Av de la Grande Armée 51
Av George V 38
Av Montaigne 38, 39

Bastille 11, 30
Bd des Capucines 44
Bd des Italiens 44
Bd Haussmann 44
Bd St-Germain 41, 58
Bd St-Michel 41, 57
Beauvais 83, 87
Bibliothèque Nationale 59
Bois de Boulogne 8, 19, 62
Bois de Vincennes 8, 62

Cabinet des Médailles et des Antiques 73
Café de la Paix 45
Canal St-Martin 16, 60
Catacombes 59
Centre Georges-Pompidou 4, 24, 71
Champ de Mars 32, 62
Champs-Elysées 8, 35, 38, 48, 50
Chantilly 87
Chartres 20, 83, 87
Château de Vincennes 62
Châtelet – see Théâtre Musical de Paris
Collège de France 57
Comédie Française 33, 75
Conciergerie 32, 66
Cour Carrée (Louvre) 51

Dôme des Invalides 32, 66

Ecole des Beaux-Arts 42, 58
Ecole Militaire 32, 66
Eiffel Tower 15, 27, 66

Faubourg St-Germain 20, 66
Fontainebleau 11, 83, 86f.
Forum des Halles 60, 79

Gare de Lyon 27, 60
Gare St-Lazare 44
Grand Palais 22, 50, 62

Hôtel Carnavalet 46, 47
Hôtel d'Almeyras 47
Hôtel de Béthune-Sully 47
Hôtel de Cluny 57, 66
Hôtel de Lamoignon 47
Hôtel de Rohan 47
Hôtel de Sandreville 47
Hôtel de Sens 66
Hôtel de Soubise 46, 47
Hôtel de Ville 46, 67

Hôtel des Invalides 32, 66
Hôtel Salé 24, 47

Île de la Cité 8, 10, 13, 53, 55
Île-St-Louis 13, 55

Jardin des Plantes 60
Jardin du Luxembourg 19, 57, 62

La Défense 4, 8, 51, 65, 83
La Grande Arche (La Défense) 4, 65
Latin Quarter 8, 13, 35, 57
Les Egouts 59
Louvre 7, 8, 10, 22, 48, 51, 63, 70ff.

Madeleine – see Ste-Marie-Madeleine
Malmaison 85
Mantes 83
Manufacture des Gobelins 60
Marais 20, 46f., 67
Marché aux Puces 60, 79
Maxim's 44
Meaux 87
Mémorial de la Déportation 55
Montmartre 10, 16, 35
Montmartre Cemetery 16, 59
Montparnasse 8, 17, 35
Mont Ste-Geneviève 8, 10
Musée de l'Armée 32, 66
Musée d'Art Moderne de la Ville de Paris 71
Musée National d'Art Moderne 24, 71
Musée des Arts Décoratifs 22, 72
Musée Balzac 72
Musée Carnavalet 22, 47, 72
Musée National de Céramique 72
Musée de Cluny 22, 52, 72
Musée Cognacq-Jay 72
Musée Delacroix 72
Musée d'Ennery 72
Musée Guimet 72
Musée Victor Hugo 72
Musée Jacquemart-André 24, 72
Musée de la Marine 72
Musée Marmottan 72
Musée de Montmartre 73
Musée d'Orsay 4, 22, 52, 73
Musée du Petit Palais 73
Musée Picasso 24, 73
Musée Rodin 24, 73

New Opera House – see Opéra Bastille

Notre-Dame-de-Paris 10, 20, 34, 53, 54, 67, 83

Odéon-Théâtre de France 33, 58, 75
Opéra (old opera house) 33, 35, 43, 67, 75
Opéra Bastille 4, 33, 67, 75
Opéra-Comique 33, 75

Palais Bourbon 21, 50, 63
Palais de Chaillot 63
Palais de l'Elysée 63
Palais du Luxembourg 19, 64
Palais Royal 18, 48
Panthéon 57, 67f.
Parc Bagatelle 19, 64
Parc de la Villette 61
Parc des Buttes-Chaumont 64
Parc du Pré Catelan 19
Parc Monceau 64
Parc Montsouris 64
Père-Lachaise Cemetery 15, 59
Petit Palais 22, 50
Place Charles-de-Gaulle 8, 50
Place de la Bastille 8, 30, 35, 37
Place de la Concorde 8, 32, 49
Place de la Madeleine 42, 44, 80
Place de l'Etoile – see Place Charles-de-Gaulle
Place de l'Odéon 57
Place de l'Opéra 43
Place des Vosges 46, 47
Place du Carrousel 48
Place du Louvre 48
Place du Tertre 17
Place Vendôme 41, 45, 81
Pompidou Centre – see Centre Georges-Pompidou
Pont Alexandre III 61
Pont Neuf 61
Pyramid (Louvre) 4, 52

Quai de Béthune 55

Rambouillet 83, 87
Ritz 45
Rue de Buci 14
Rue de Grenelle 21
Rue de Lappe 37
Rue de Lille 21
Rue de la Cité 53
Rue de la Paix 45
Rue de Rivoli 8
Rue de Varenne 21
Rue des Francs-Bourgeois 46f.
Rue du Faubourg St-Honoré 38f., 41
Rue du Paradis 41

Rue du Parc Royal 47
Rue Lafitte 41
Rue Lepic 14
Rue Mouffetard 14
Rue Royale 44
Rue St-Honoré 41, 45

Sacré-Coeur 8, 16, 68
Salle Favart – see Opéra-Comique
Sceaux 87
Senlis 20, 83, 87
Sorbonne 8, 10, 57
Square de l'Île-de-France 55
Square du Vert Galant 55
Sainte-Chapelle 20, 53, 54, 70, 83

Ste-Marie-Madeleine 44, 49, 67
St-Denis (cathedral) 10, 20, 68, 83
St-Denis (district) 81
St-Etienne-du-Mont 69
St-Eustache 20, 34, 69
St-Germain-des-Prés 8, 14, 35, 58, 69
St-Germain-en-Laye 83, 85f.
St-Germain-l'Auxerrois 20, 69
St-Julien-le-Pauvre 57, 69
St-Louis-en-l'Île 55, 69
St-Séverin 13, 34, 57, 69
St-Sulpice 58, 69

Théâtre de l'Est Parisien (TEP) 34, 75
Théâtre Musical de Paris (Théâtre du Châtelet) 33, 75
Théâtre National de Chaillot 34, 75
Théâtre National de l'Odéon – see Odéon-Théâtre de France
Tour Maine-Montparnasse 17, 61
Tour St-Jacques 70
Tuileries 8, 49, 63

Val-de-Grâce 70
Vaux-le-Vicomte 87
Versailles 11, 83ff.